bulletproof

HEALING AFTER GUN VIOLENCE & TRAUMA

A Guide for Survivors, Caregivers, and Clinicians

HEALING AFTER GUN VIOLENCE & TRAUMA

A Guide for Survivors, Caregivers, and Clinicians

Jill Mcmahon, LPC
GRIEF AND TRAUMA SPECIALIST

Niche Pressworks
Indianapolis, IN

BULLETPROOF

Copyright © 2024 by JILL MCMAHON

To respect the privacy of my clients who have shared their stories with me, I have changed some names and identifying details. Stories, in some instances, are composites of multiple clients and experiences to maintain anonymity.

Bulletproof, and the information provided by Jill McMahon, is intended for educational and informational purposes only. It is not a substitute for the advice, diagnosis, or treatment regarding medical or mental health conditions. Although Jill McMahon is a licensed therapist, the views expressed in this book or any related content should not be taken as medical or psychiatric advice. Always consult your physician or mental health provider before making any decisions related to your physical or mental health.

For permission to reprint portions of this content or for bulk purchases, contact Jill@JillMcmahonCounseling.com

Author Photograph by: Bekki Lawson Photography

Published by Niche Pressworks: NichePressworks.com
Indianapolis, IN

ISBN
Hardcover: 978-1-962956-20-8
Paperback: 978-1-962956-21-5
eBook: 978-1-962956-19-2

Library of Congress Cataloging-in-Publication Data on File at lccn.loc.gov

The views expressed herein are solely those of the author and do not necessarily reflect the views of the publisher.

To those impacted by gun violence and sudden loss ...
I see you! No words are enough other than
I am so incredibly sorry for your pain.

To caregivers, this is complicated and scary for you, too.
I validate your important role. We appreciate you.

To mental health professionals, your role
in healing is a mighty one. We need your
knowledge, your compassion, and your guidance.
Don't forget to take care of yourselves along the way.

Table of Contents

Real Talk About Healing

I have known Jill McMahon for the entirety of her remarkable twenty-plus-year career. In fact, Jill and I started our careers at nearly the same time. Despite the thousands of miles that have often separated us, our experiences have been strikingly similar. For Jill, it was Columbine in 1999. For me, it was the Washington Navy Yard shooting in 2013. And for both of us, it was the hundreds and (for Jill) thousands of survivors in between.

My name is Michelle Palmer, and I'm a licensed clinical social worker. For the past eleven years, I have been the executive director of the Wendt Center for Loss and Healing. The Wendt Center is located in Washington, DC, which some may know as the former "murder capitol" of the United States. In 2025, the Center will have been helping communities for fifty years by providing specialized mental health care to people navigating the impact of grief and/or trauma — our expertise being the intersection of both. During our decades of service, we have worked with tens of thousands of people whose lives have been irrevocably changed by gun violence.

I tell you all of that because I know from what I speak, and so does Jill. *Bulletproof* is a refreshing, real-talk book about the similarities and differences in the experiences of gun violence survivors. It explains the biology of trauma in a way that you don't have to be a scientist or a therapist to understand. It provides perspective from "both sides of the couch" because Jill is a clinician who has been in this work for over two decades and is, herself, a survivor of gun violence. The stories, including Jill's, are similar and yet different. Hopefully, they will offer you, the reader, anchors on the way to healing. *Bulletproof* offers information you can reference or sit with as you learn to navigate the healing process that is unique to gun violence survivors.

Additionally, *Bulletproof* is a practical, no-nonsense book for counseling and social work programs. It provides essential details needed as part of their training curriculum. Until we prioritize ending gun violence, we *must* prioritize healing from it.

Jill, thank you for entrusting me with the foreword to this treasure of a book.

Always,
Michelle Palmer, LICSW
Executive Director, Wendt Center for Loss and Healing

Everything Changed

One of the most anxiety-provoking moments of my life was buckling my newborn into the car as we left the hospital. When I arrived at that same building two days before, this baby was securely nestled inside my body. Now, a mere forty-eight hours later, I felt bewildered and a bit terrified when I realized that these professionals were really going to hand me this tiny, fragile, seven-pound human and fully expected that I would know how to care for it.

As my husband and I pulled away from the hospital with our infant, I was in too much awe (and fear) to pay attention to anything outside the car. We didn't notice the stream of ambulances coming into the bay as we pulled away. We didn't even have the car radio on. We were singularly focused on this sleeping baby boy. Was he buckled in too tight? Could he breathe easily? Would we make it home before he started screaming? My maternal instincts were only concerned with the speed my husband was driving and the thought of kicking him if he took the next bump too fast.

Four minutes later, as we pulled into our driveway (yes, I was *that* concerned about a drive that took less than five minutes), we were obsessed with this new life and focused on nothing else. I walked slowly to the front door so my husband could wrangle the Labrador retriever waiting inside, holding his collar to make sure he didn't jump on me or the bundle in my arms. We were still unaware of anything except this incredible little life we had created and just brought home for the first time.

That innocent moment was short-lived as the neighbor's teenage son came rushing toward us. He was winded and in a hurry. "Can I come in? Can I use your phone? I need to call my mom! I can't get in the house! She's gonna be worried!"

None of this was registering. Why was he home at midday on a Tuesday? Wasn't he supposed to be in school? Maybe I was just in a baby fog.

At that moment, the world we had been shutting out came to life. In the distance, we faintly heard the wail of ambulances, but it was seeing this young man's panic that set our hearts racing. He was speaking quickly, almost babbling, sharing details we didn't really comprehend. Of course, we brought him into the house and led him to the phone. It was obvious that something was happening and that he needed his mom.

Seconds after he hung up, our phone rang. "Are you okay?" my mother-in-law asked.

We were better than okay! We had just brought the most beautiful human being ever created home with us!

She said, "Turn on the TV." And that's when our hearts dropped, and the sirens became even louder.

On April 20, 1999, we resided in Littleton, Colorado, and Columbine High School was four miles from our home. As we were bringing our precious new life home for the first time, ambulances were driving into that same hospital with children from the Columbine High School shooting whose lives were ending or irreparably altered.

In those moments, as we were learning the joy and terror of new beginnings, many other parents in the Columbine community were learning that their children's lives were ending as a result of gun violence.

About Me

I've thought a lot about Columbine and that moment — about the difficult balance between hope and devastation. Like you, I am, first and foremost, human — trying to sustain myself, love and mold my family, and make a difference in this world. I am a mental health professional who has devoted my life to sitting with people in their darkest moments and attempting, inch by inch, to help them "survive."

I am also a childhood gun violence survivor and gun violence prevention advocate. I understand, both professionally and personally, the confusion, pain, and disorientation that weaves in and out of a survivor's new reality.

When Columbine happened, I was a new mom and midway through a graduate program in counseling psychology. I planned to be a marriage and family therapist, but soon realized that wasn't the right path.

After Columbine, I continued my program and started an internship with the Wendt Center for Loss and Healing, a nationally recognized organization specializing in grief and trauma located in Washington, D.C. This experience was pivotal and changed the direction of my professional future.

As part of my internship, I worked at the medical examiner's office, helping families identify the bodies of their loved ones and also working with young children who had suddenly lost family members. However, the most memorable work was my time spent with survivors of suicide. That term, if it's unfamiliar to you, is used to describe the friends and family members who have been left behind after a suicide has occurred.

After one night with these suicide survivors who were dealing with unimaginable grief, I knew that I had found my purpose. These individuals are often grossly misunderstood, and I wanted to help change that.

Since that day, I've spent over twenty years of my life working in trauma and grief, specifically working with friends and family members impacted by a loss to suicide. I've held hands with family members just hours after a traumatic death occurred. I've visited homes while the medical examiner's van was still in the driveway. I have facilitated goodbyes between mothers and sons while one is in a body bag. I've sat on the floor of my office with clients in the months (and even years) after a loved one has died and just allowed them to wail.

Gun-related trauma and sudden loss have played a strong role in my professional life — and in my personal life as well.

Bulletproof and You

Bulletproof is the first book of its kind written specifically for people impacted by gun violence and traumatic loss. I started writing this book to help people heal by sharing what I've learned after working with thousands of trauma victims with unique experiences.

Maybe you are a gun violence survivor. Maybe you've lost a loved one to gun violence, suicide, or sudden death (homicide, car accident — the list is long).

This book is also for caregivers — those who sit on the sidelines, feeling lost about how they can truly help or feeling like they can't deeply understand what a loved one is going through because they haven't lived that horrific event themselves. Caregivers can be family and friends, but they can also be neighbors, coworkers, doctors, or anyone who is committed to your health (physical, mental, or emotional).

Maybe you haven't had a gun pointed in your direction, but you've been a little too close to the aftermath of a gun-related event. You are a secondary victim, and there are many of you — more and more every day.

Bulletproof is for each of you.

What This Book Is Not

Before we get too far along, I also want to explain some of what *Bulletproof* is not. I want to be up-front about what you can expect in this book.

- *Bulletproof* is not a political debate about firearm rights or ownership, which plenty of other publications cover. *Bulletproof is about healing.*
- *Bulletproof* is not meant to be an academic or clinical guide for overcoming PTSD or other complex mental health disorders. *It's meant to speak with you, not talk over you.*
- *Bulletproof* may not be a right fit for veterans of war or those who have engaged in combat. These experiences come with complexities and require guidance different from what will be covered here. *I've included a list of general and veteran-related resources in the appendix.*

What This Book Is

Bulletproof is a guide meant to connect with you on a human level about surviving trauma. I will intentionally write and speak plainly and clearly about a tough topic. From detailing the most common reactions experienced after gun violence to explaining how individuals can overcome and even overpower this pain, I will take you through it all step by step. Some of the important topics discussed include:

- Exploring how gun violence, suicide loss, and sudden trauma affect both the mind and the body.
- Creating a roadmap that details how to heal, overcome, and overpower the life-altering impact of gun-related trauma.
- Providing an overview of specific practices and approaches survivors have successfully used to heal from their trauma.
- Crafting an educational guide for mental health professionals that provides suggestions and best practices to be used when working with gun violence survivors and trauma victims.

What to Expect

If you've picked up this book (or added it to your Amazon cart), I suspect that you, in some way, can relate to the title. Whatever your reason, stick with me. I will walk you through it all. I am asking you to trust me and devote time to my words — time that I know is valuable. I don't take that time lightly. Nor do I take you or your experiences lightly. Instead, I want to sit alongside you as you read from chapter to chapter.

I will explain and contextualize how these types of trauma shape our thought processes after an event. I will suggest ways to support yourself and those you love or work with. I will remind you that there *is* life after this trauma and, damn, that life can be *good!*

Read that again. Life after experiencing trauma due to gun violence can be good again.

If you've picked up this book because you've been traumatically impacted, that can't be undone. You can, however, heal.

I hope to show you that your spirit is bulletproof!

— Jill

Important Note: *Gun violence is a tough topic. Some of the information we'll discuss is easier to digest in small doses, and that's okay. Don't judge yourself if you need to read a chapter and then set this book down for a while. Come back to these pages when you are ready.*

chapter 1

Gun Violence Epidemic

We do learn so much about ourselves in our experiences.
But also, know that it shouldn't have happened.
This was not a lesson you needed to learn.

—JORDAN PICKELL

On the outside, Laura had everything going for her. She was a hard-working 24-year-old law student with all the accolades and awards of an exemplary professional-to-be. She had a boyfriend who adored her and friends who surrounded her with love. Yet, on the inside, Laura felt anxious, tired, and irritable. Even with her extensive support system, she felt unable to share her internal struggles or the fact that she rarely had a good night's sleep. She knew she needed to share her family's story. She knew she needed to be honest with her friends and talk to her mentor about what she was experiencing. But, when push came to shove, she was unable to speak the words.

Nearly two years before, Laura's mother had shot herself in front of her father. Now, Laura feared the pain that would be associated with even whispering details of the events of her mother's suicide. She was struggling to manage the trauma and reached out to me.

I had met with Laura's father during the year following the suicide. I heard stories of her brothers' struggles since that devastating day, but during that time, there was little discussion of how Laura was doing. She was focused on holding the family together and did not seek support for herself.

However, Laura had now hit the invisible wall that many suicide and gun violence survivors encounter. She had social and emotional support many people do not have, yet she was still incapable of sharing her horrors with others or finding a way to heal.

Laura is not alone.

I chose Laura's story to begin this chapter because it's time to expand the definition of who we're talking about when we talk about gun violence survivors. It also includes those left behind — families, friends, and communities.

Some people may not initially think suicide survivors are also gun violence survivors. Yet more than 57 percent of gun deaths in the United States are the result of suicide.[1] That makes the loved ones of those who die by suicide also gun violence survivors. And they experience similar physical and emotional reactions to the trauma.

The impact of gun violence affects more Americans than ever before, which makes it so important to understand what it is and who it impacts.

Impact of Gun Violence

Gun violence is violence committed with the use of a firearm. It may be homicide, assault with a deadly weapon, suicide, or attempted suicide. It also includes the act of being threatened with a gun and fearing for one's personal safety.

As a matter of fact, one in five adults (20 percent) say a family member has been injured by a gun. Nineteen percent say a family member has been killed by a gun, including suicide.[2]

THE NUMBERS

Let's put the waders on and step into the nitty gritty of what gun violence looks like at the time of this publication. It's not pretty.

A March 2023 poll by the Kaiser Family Foundation reported that 54 percent of US adults reported that either they, personally, or a family member had been impacted by a gun-related incident, including being threatened by a gun, witnessing a shooting, or being injured or killed by a gun.

The same poll noted the following statistics:

- 21 percent reported being threatened with a gun
- 17 percent had witnessed someone being shot
- 4 percent had been injured by a gun
- 4 percent had shot a gun in self-defense

More than half the population has reported being impacted by gun violence in some way. These events affect the way we view the world and how we live our daily lives. Exposure to gun violence is known to increase rates of depression, anxiety, post-traumatic stress disorder, and suicide. It can also lead to an increased risk of cardiovascular disease. And this growing exposure shows no signs of slowing down.

CHILDREN AND GUNS

In 2020, guns overtook motor vehicle accidents as the leading cause of death in children ages one to seventeen.[3]

Let that sink in. More children die as a result of gun violence than car accidents.

And three million children are directly exposed to gun violence every year, resulting in death, injury, and lasting trauma.[4] For my budding mental health professionals who are reading this chapter, many of those children will be your future clients. The psychological damage to the developing brain from gun violence exposure will have lasting effects that parents, professionals, and society are likely to see for years, if not decades.

In 2020, guns overtook motor vehicle accidents as the leading cause of death in children ages 1–17.

GROWING UP AFTER TRAUMA

The psychological impact of gun violence on children is long lasting and changes as the child and their brain develop. This is particularly true as they gain a greater understanding of their surroundings and begin to question the safety of their environment. In other words, if a child is four years old when first exposed to gun violence, they will understand the same event very differently when they turn eight, twelve, sixteen, twenty, and so on until the brain is fully developed between the ages twenty-four and twenty-eight.

For this reason, it is important to provide consistent and age-appropriate support for children who have been exposed to gun violence. Counseling or trauma work may not be a one-time event for these children. Instead, it may be something that needs to be repeated at different stages of their development.

Let's use Laura as an example. Although she wasn't a young child at the time of her mother's suicide (she was a senior in college), her brain was still developing. She accompanied her dad to his first session with me just a few months after her mother's death. At that time, Laura was still in shock and more concerned about her surviving parent than herself, which is common in children of trauma. During that initial stage, she was angry and confused. Laura wanted to push it all into a mental box and close the lid tightly so she could go on living what were supposed to be some of the most joyous years of her life.

Fast forward to when Laura contacted me asking for individual help. Her brain's comprehension of her mother's death was quite different from how it had originally processed what had happened. Initially, she felt sadness, confusion, and anger. Two years later, she reported feelings of abandonment, guilt, and overwhelm.

In those years, Laura's brain had developed further, resulting in a different understanding of the event. This illustrates the importance of processing trauma separately at each developmental stage. We'll examine the impact of trauma on the brain in greater detail in a later chapter.

RACE AND GUN VIOLENCE

Gun violence does not impact us equally. People of color in the United States are disproportionately impacted by gun violence.

- Black adults are about *twice as likely* as White adults to have a family member who has been killed by a gun and/or to have personally witnessed someone being shot.[5]
- One-fifth of Hispanic adults have personally witnessed someone being shot.
- One-third of Black and Hispanic adults say they worry "every day" or "almost every day" that they or someone they love will be a victim of gun violence, compared to one in ten (or just 10 percent) of White adults.

While researching for this book, I interviewed a member of the Rockefeller Institute of Government's Regional Gun Violence Research Consortium, a coalition of gun violence researchers and practitioners working to shift the current gun violence trend by educating policymakers and the public.

During that conversation, I was connected with Brooklynn Hitchens, an assistant professor at the University of Maryland. Hitchens is a sociologist and community-engaged researcher whose work focuses on Black women and girls, specifically those who have been victimized or are gun violence survivors.

Hitchens' work highlights the disproportionate impact of gun violence on Black women and girls. She describes how Black households are frequently female-headed, and Black male homicide victims are often survived by partners, including girlfriends or the mothers of their children.[6]

When this occurs, these women are forced to take over making funeral arrangements, settling debts, and caring for those left behind. In addition to the emotional trauma of losing a loved one, Hitchens explains how urban Black women and girls often experience economic hardship due to the loss of household income and become responsible for more domestic demands. The challenges posed by this daily struggle and hardship have been termed the "second killing." Hitchens' research creates a clear image of the damage and complexity of gun violence, particularly in low-income, urban Black communities.

Gun violence impacts us all, yet not evenly. Some are left behind to burden more than emotional distress.

SECONDARY SURVIVOR STORY

If you've been a bystander or are a family member, friend, or first responder, it's crucial to acknowledge what you have witnessed. There is no need to compare yourself to a victim by thinking, "Well, I wasn't the one who was fearing for my life. What do I have to complain about? My experience is nothing in comparison."

Trauma is an individual experience and looks different for different people. What you witnessed is not typical and is absolutely difficult to process. It is okay to ask for assistance with that processing. This really hit home for me when I received a call several years ago. A woman called me because her husband was in distress, and she didn't know who else to turn to for help.

Her husband was the maintenance worker at a local apartment complex. The week before she called, he had been tasked with cleaning and painting one of the units after the tenant had taken his life by firearm. She described how his response to what he'd seen had become concerning. She wasn't sure how best to support him.

She told me that he struggled to sleep, was overly emotional, and just seemed detached from life. She explained that her husband felt it wasn't fair to complain about his emotional discomfort because there were others who were more directly impacted by this trauma.

He was not validating his own experience, yet he was obviously suffering.

It's okay to validate your experience when you witness, see, and hear things that are difficult to process. It is okay to ask for help to clear those images from your memory. You, too, have been impacted.

*In the United States, over half of all adults
have experienced a gun-related incident.
One in five have been personally threatened
with a gun or have had a family member
who has been killed by a gun.*

THE RIPPLE EFFECT

You don't have to face a gun to experience the aftermath. Maybe you weren't at the mall, hiding in the classroom, or near the fired shots. You can still be impacted by gun violence. It's important that we begin to acknowledge how far-reaching the emotional and psychological effects of gun violence really are.

We are seeing more and more community members stressed out by traumatic events they didn't even experience firsthand. In the mental health field, we call this "secondary trauma" and "vicarious trauma." Let me break those definitions down for you.

Secondary trauma is the distress that occurs when an individual has been indirectly exposed to trauma. It can occur by simply hearing disturbing details and descriptions from a trauma survivor. It is also sometimes experienced by the caretaker of an individual who has been victimized.

Individuals experiencing secondary trauma can feel the emotional impact of the trauma, experiencing symptoms like difficulty managing emotions and feeling emotionally numb or shut down. They also might have difficulty sleeping, leaving them feeling fatigued, irritable, and easily distracted. Similar to direct victims of trauma, they, too, may lose a sense of safety, worry constantly, and feel unexplained physical aches and pains.

The term vicarious trauma typically refers to individuals in professions with repeated exposure to trauma, including EMTs, firefighters, law enforcement, crisis responders, nurses, and mental health professionals. Common reactions to vicarious trauma are the same as above, but they can include professional and personal burnout as well.

When you include the ripple effect — people who are affected by secondary and vicarious trauma — the number of individuals who have been impacted by gun violence grows exponentially. Their worldview has been shifted due to gun violence, and I suspect that their distress is not accurately represented in the statistics presented above. If that, in fact, is true, the impact of gun violence on our society is one that very few of us can escape.

IT'S CRITICAL

The urgency of matters related to gun violence can be seen in the numbers. Statistics illustrate trends, and these trends show us the enormity of the gun violence problem in the United States as well as the massive number of people who have been impacted. From innocent bystanders to children to people of color, gun violence leaves a path of trauma and destruction in its wake.

fast facts

- Gun violence is violence committed with the use of a firearm. It includes homicide, assault with a deadly weapon, suicide, and attempted suicide. It is the act of being threatened by a firearm and fearing for one's safety.

- Over fifty percent of our population has reported being impacted by gun violence in some way.

- More children die as a result of gun violence than car accidents.

- Children exposed to gun violence will understand their trauma differently at different ages and will need support as they grow and their brain develops.

- Exposure to violence has been known to increase rates of depression, anxiety, post-traumatic stress disorder, and suicide.

- People of color in the United States are disproportionately impacted by gun violence.

- Secondary trauma/vicarious trauma is the distress that occurs when an individual has been indirectly exposed to trauma. This population is at risk for emotional burnout.

Mental Health Professionals

Throughout the book, you'll find sections written specifically for mental health professionals. It's meant to be an educational guide and to help shine a light on this growing population of clients and their need for real understanding, compassion, and know-how.

The effect of gun violence on our culture is prevalent. It is important to acknowledge it is unique compared to other types of trauma. Your clients deserve knowledgeable, individual care that applies to their specific experience rather than being placed in the same group as those suffering other losses and experiences.

Gun violence survivors seek support because they feel misunderstood and isolated. Building trust in a therapeutic relationship may take time for a survivor. Don't rush the process — being a stable source of support for them will prove invaluable.

If you don't have experience working with gun violence survivors, it's okay to seek consultation with practitioners who have. Ask them to support you. Use this book as a helpful resource, and remember, we all had that "first" with a client.

Expand your understanding of who is impacted by gun violence to include suicide survivors, first responders, caregivers, and even you — mental health providers. Realize that not all of these subgroups have the same support available to them. Each client comes to you with their own unique history, coping skills, and family support. Acknowledge these differences and plan your treatment accordingly. No client is the same as another.

Important Note: The next chapter will probably be the most graphic and challenging to get through. It is dedicated to sharing survivor stories. Retelling these stories is not meant to create pain, but instead, it is meant to be real about survivors' experiences. This can help remind survivors that they are not alone and help those who haven't been impacted better understand what it's like to be someone who has. Until we all have a greater understanding of what gun violence survivors live with, we can't genuinely and effectively help them heal.

chapter 2

Gun Violence Survivors

Sometimes in life, a sudden situation, a moment in time, alters your whole life, forever changing the road ahead.

—AHMAD ARDALAN

This book isn't a guide about how to tiptoe around trauma — neither yours nor your loved ones. Its purpose is to get in the weeds and be real. It's an opportunity to validate the experiences of those who have lived through it and create a greater understanding for those who haven't. Making these connections helps us understand the impact of gun violence, and that is what makes this chapter necessary.

Surviving gun violence means many things, so it's important to paint an accurate picture of what it looks like and not to candy-coat the details. We can't begin to explore paths to healing until we unearth the reality of the mind and body's response to trauma.

In this chapter, we'll read the stories of people who have survived gun violence. Each story is unique. Each of these survivors experienced a different trauma. Perhaps one will resonate with you, or maybe none of them will because your story has its own twists and turns that make it familiar only to you.

What is important to notice, however, are the similarities in responses to trauma that are shared by these survivors. Do these responses sound familiar to you? If you haven't experienced a sudden loss or life-altering traumatic event yourself, they may not. But please take note here of the themes and feelings of each story. It may provide some insight into what loved ones or acquaintances have gone through and allow for greater empathy for them and their struggles.

***A Word of Caution:** For some, the stories that follow may be triggering. The events shared are real and, therefore, traumatic. We will not go into graphic detail about gun violence events; however, they are survivor stories and will be emotionally powerful.*

If at any time you feel like reading these stories is too painful for you, it is okay to set this book down for a while or move on to chapters about how this trauma affects the brain and body. Then, come back if and when you feel ready.

Jill – Child Survivor of Gun Violence

I was six years old on that summer day when my mom and I were walking out of the mall. We had just dropped off my sister and her friend, and I remember feeling disappointed that I didn't at least get an Orange Julius out of the trip.

As we walked through the parking lot toward our Lincoln Continental, I remember two handsome men walking toward us. They looked like clean-cut surfer boys, wearing button-up Izod shirts and O.P. shorts while keeping their eyes hidden behind trendy aviator sunglasses.

The men struck up a conversation with my mom. From my vantage point, at all of four feet tall, I recall them telling my mom they had a flat tire and pointing to their car just a few parking spots down from ours. They asked my mom if she would give them a ride to their friend's house, just a couple of miles away. I remember the look of hesitance on my mom's face. "Did you try the gas station on the other side of the mall?" she asked. They assured her they had and that there was no one there who could help them. But, if they could get to their friend's house, he would take them to get their tire repaired.

From my lower viewpoint, I noticed the folded-up newspaper soon after the men approached us. I could see a small, silver pistol in between the pages of that newspaper, which one of the men was holding near his waist. I thought I knew exactly what that gun was for. Surely, he had a young son at home and bought this toy for him while at the mall. After several questions and much back and forth, my mom, though feeling apprehensive, eventually relented. These men were so polite. They were so clean-cut. What could go wrong?

The man with the newspaper got in the back seat with me while his partner took the passenger seat up front with my mom. After our car left the mall parking lot, the men began giving my mom directions to the destination. I remember looking out the window, watching the trees go by, and knowing exactly where we were. My big brother had a friend who lived down one of these streets. We'd gone there to pick him up from time to time.

"Take a left here, on Primrose Street," the man in the passenger seat told my mom. We were just a few miles from the mall. Once we turned onto this quiet neighborhood street, everything changed. The man in the front gestured to a house, said it belonged to their friend, and asked my mom to pull over.

A FRIGHTENING TURN

Then the man next to me said words that I will never forget. In a flat voice that I can still hear, he said, "Ma'am, we have a problem back here." The look on my mom's face in the rearview mirror as she saw him holding the gun to my head was almost more alarming to me than the feel of the metal. My biggest fear in the hours that followed was that these men would kill my mother.

Moments later, the man in the front seat pulled out a switchblade and held it to my mom's side. I saw the knife briefly between the two front seats. The two men directed my mom to drive to a bank and withdraw all that she could without attracting too much attention. My mom's only frantic plea was for my safety.

"Please. I have a friend who lives nearby. Can we *please* drop my daughter off? Please don't hurt her. She doesn't need to be here. Please!" She must have made that request three times. The response was always simply "no." When we pulled up to the bank, my mom was instructed to park, and then the man in back with me escorted my mom inside with the gun in his pocket.

I stayed in the car with the gentleman who was sitting in the front seat. He was trying to chat lightly with me. "How's your summer? Do you like to draw?" I was an obedient child, so I answered. I never cried. Instead, I smiled, played nice, and just waited. I figured that my job in those moments was to be a "good girl." Maybe if I was a good girl, my mom and I would make it home alive.

It felt like time was both flying by and moving at a snail's pace. The next thing I knew, we were all back in the car together, and my mom was driving to another bank. The kidnappers were demanding more money.

As I looked out the window, I noticed the sky was getting darker outside. I sat in the back seat and schemed ways in which I could successfully free us from the kidnappers and save my mom from being hurt. Again, that was my only true concern — they would hurt my mom. I fantasized about kicking the kidnapper next to me in his "private parts." I'd seen it in the movies. The bad guy gets kneed in the nuts, instantly bends over in anguish, and the victim gets away. I was six years old, so I quickly realized that I didn't have the courage to go through with it myself.

At the second bank, only the drive-thru was open. "Don't say anything funny or do anything stupid," one of the kidnappers was saying to my mom. The weapons in the car were tucked away so that the teller in the bank window wouldn't see anything out of the ordinary. This was just another transaction for her as she looked at us through the window, smiling and conversing with my mom. I prayed the teller had superhuman powers and could see what was really going on in our car. My mom was less chatty. She was nervous. She was doing what she was told, taking the money out of the drawer and placing the envelope of cash at her side before driving off.

JUST KEEP GOING

"Drive towards that neighborhood," the man in front gestured with his chin. "Just keep going." My mom awaited her next instruction, not sure what the next step would be or what was next for us. We were in the middle of suburbia, and an elementary school was ahead. Because it was well past school hours, there was no one on campus. The school property butted up to a small community golf course. "Right here. Stop in front of the school," the man in the front directed. "Now place the car in park, and both of you get out." Sternly this time, he said, "Walk straight ahead for ten minutes. Don't turn around or speak to anyone! And leave your wallet."

My mom grabbed my hand, and we walked straight forward, almost as if we were robots. We didn't dare look behind us or even side to side — instead, we walked like our bodies were rigid and focused.

When we reached the back wall of the school, my mom grabbed me and turned the corner, out of sight from where the car was parked. This is when she started screaming. I mean screaming! Another sound I will never forget. Children don't typically hear their parents scream in primal fear and desperation.

There were golfers just on the other side of a chain-link fence. When they heard my mom, they instantly dropped their clubs and came running toward us. I remember being lifted over the fence and swept into the safety of a small clubhouse. I remember sitting on a stranger's lap. He was a sweet gentleman; he had a grandfatherly warmth to him. He gave me candy. My mom was near but was frantically answering a hundred questions and attempting to regain composure. I was always in her eyesight. Soon, the police were there. There was a flurry of activity, and lots of questions were asked. But I knew we were safe. My mom was safe.

THE AFTERMATH

In the months that passed, we didn't really discuss the events of that day. At least they weren't discussed with me. I've always suspected there was a "if we don't talk about it, it won't damage Jill" kind of safety plan. That attitude would be fairly common for parenting in that day. My parents were just doing their best with the skills they had. At that time, no one knew much about the impact of trauma on children, and the concept of Adverse Childhood Experiences (ACEs) wasn't introduced until the mid-1990s.

I imagine my siblings and dad had their own traumatic responses to this event, but I wasn't privy to those either. A sense of safety was stolen from all of us on that day. In my young mind, I figured that since we didn't talk about it, everyone and everything must be okay. Little did I know that this was just the beginning of my trauma processing.

Jennifer – Adult Survivor of Gun Violence

"I should probably grab my Kleenex," Jennifer says before we start our interview. I met Jennifer twelve years ago when we both served as board members for Arizonans for Gun Safety. She was a strong personality, sometimes gruff but incredibly passionate. If you had to go to battle, she's the friend you wanted by your side. So when some of her first words to me during our Zoom call were, "Let me grab my Kleenex," I was caught off guard. As the scene expanded in real time, Jennifer rolled back from the camera. Her wheelchair moved out of sight as she went to grab a box of tissues.

I'd never previously asked Jennifer about the night she was shot. It was kind of an unspoken agreement, as if all that mattered was that we understood one another as survivors. The details weren't important. But before I dove in and asked her about the event that paralyzed her, I wanted to know what Jennifer's daily life was like before she was shot.

Jennifer was an athletic go-getter. A divorced mom with a twelve-year-old boy, she was a successful massage therapist who spent her days focusing on what makes the body work and helping others alleviate the pains they held — ironic, considering her fate. Jennifer was in a loving relationship with a partner who held many of the same interests, most of them adventure oriented. "David and I would wake up on a typical day, share a yogurt, and set out to run up a local mountain (making sure to stop at every station to do our push-ups or hip dips). Once we made it home, there would be a round of 1,000 kicks to the kickbag before we would even start our day." David owned a karate studio, and Jennifer was a newly certified instructor.

The week before the shooting, Jennifer and David were on a deep-sea diving trip in Fiji. It was during this trip that Jennifer finally accepted David's marriage proposal. He had asked plenty of times before, but Jennifer said there was just something about this trip — its atmosphere, the beauty of it, and him. It compelled her to finally say "Yes." Through my computer screen, I see Jennifer giggle as she calls David "an amazing Adonis of a man." You can see the reflection on her face as she recalls those warm, safe, romantic moments with him. Forty-eight hours later, their lives would change forever.

Still floating from their incredible trip together, Jennifer and David returned to their reality in Phoenix, Arizona. On the first day back, they both worked a full day and taught karate that night, so they decided to stop and grab some Mexican food to take home. This was nothing out of the ordinary for them. There was a restaurant nearby where they would often stop for takeout.

LIFE CHANGED IN AN INSTANT

That night, however, as they were pulling into the parking lot of that familiar restaurant, their car was sideswiped by another vehicle. Seconds later, Jennifer heard the gunshots. She recounts those moments frame by frame — ducking under the dashboard as much as she could from the passenger seat and David screaming, "Get down!" as she attempted to dial 9-1-1. She recalls feeling David throw his body over hers and still hearing the shots overhead. She remembers confusion and fear — so much fear. It was all happening so fast and yet also somehow in slow motion.

The bullets stopped at some point, and Jennifer was still crouched low. She felt the truck move forward and realized that David was attempting to escape, but she could see that his body was slumped over the steering wheel, and he wasn't moving. That is when Jennifer heard two more shots, and, this time, she was hit in the back. She describes this feeling as "the worst fire imaginable," traveling up and down her spine — a feeling she will never forget.

After being shot, Jennifer was still able to reach over and grab the steering wheel, steering the truck into a palm tree. She needed to make a split-second decision: hit the tree or swerve and hit the building behind the tree, which could injure innocent people. Jennifer chose the tree. As scary as that was, she knew the truck would at least come to a stop.

New fear arose once the truck was no longer in motion. "Are the shooters coming after us?" "Will the next bullet be the kill shot?" In these moments, one thought was consistent from beginning to end — her son. She desperately wanted him to know how much she loved him. Moments later, EMTs responded to the scene. Her first statement was a plea, "Please tell my son that I love him!" Then, they rushed her and David into ambulances headed to separate hospitals.

RECOVERY

After that night, Jennifer spent nearly five months in the hospital. The shooting was an ongoing investigation, and the perpetrators had not been apprehended. Jennifer was kept hidden in a specific hospital wing. Her name was not listed as a current patient, and no one was allowed to visit. Jennifer was separated from David, who had also survived. Due to the severity of his injuries, he was taken to a different local trauma hospital. She was disconnected from her life, but most catastrophically, she was paralyzed.

In Jennifer's words, "Everything changed." During this unbelievably challenging time, she suffered incredible loss — the loss of her home, her social circle, and being a caregiver for her child. She lost her sense of safety for years to come. However, Jennifer talks about how the hardest thing to overcome was losing her self-image. "It defines everything," she says. "People were hesitant to approach me, almost shy. That type of response to you creates a mirror image. I just kept thinking, 'Wow, I must really be f*&@d up!'"

It took the next nineteen years for Jennifer to feel like she had taken back control of her life.

Hannah (Teen Survivor) and Nicole (Parent Caregiver)

In December 2013, Nicole was a fifth-grade teacher in Centennial, Colorado. She vividly remembers the day one of her students rushed toward her in the hallway, saying, "Ms. Larsen, Ms. Larsen, there was a shooting at my brothers' high school!" There was panic in young Robbie's voice. Nicole knew that his brothers went to Arapahoe High School, and so did her own daughter, Hannah.

That's when the world went into hyperdrive for Nicole. She immediately called Hannah but got no answer. She then called her husband and her parents. Her husband had heard about the shooting and was on his way to the school. Again, Nicole tried to get ahold of Hannah with no success. Nicole remembers that it felt like they were the last family to hear from their child. Nearly an hour passed with no contact.

While Nicole was desperately trying to find out if her daughter was safe, she was also responsible for her class of twenty-five fifth-grade students. The elementary school where Nicole worked was four miles from Arapahoe High School, and all schools in the district were locked down, including hers.

Nicole recalls how the children in her classroom were confused and crying. She was torn between supporting and calming them and worrying about the safety of her own child.

HANNAH

Meanwhile, Hannah was huddled in a corner of the high school theater. As a child who struggled with sensory issues, the blaring fire alarm that was screaming on repeat was wearing her down. She recalls trying to "stay small" and remain quiet. Hannah, a freshman, remembered hearing the first gunshot and thinking that one of the upperclassmen must have dropped their textbook in the hallway. Then several loud bangs followed — the Molotov cocktail bombs the shooter set off in the library. Hannah was born and raised in Littleton, Colorado. She knew about Columbine. With each loud bang, she knew something was wrong, and it was serious.

In the hour before Nicole made contact with Hannah, they had learned that the shooter was dead, and the "event" had ended within minutes. However, Hannah was still hiding in the theater, alarms screaming in her ears. The authorities needed to make sure the shooter was acting alone, so she was told to stay put until the scene could be cleared. Nicole did the best she could to support Hannah via phone while she waited for the police to escort her from the building.

At the time, they didn't know that "clearing a scene" could take hours or that the tactical teams releasing the students would enter each room, one by one, holding semiautomatic weapons. While many other students had been led out on the football field or placed on busses to travel to safety, Hannah remained in that dark theater. She continued her efforts to stay small and stay quiet.

These were the moments that Hannah would need help recovering from for years to come.

BEING HANNAH'S CAREGIVER

"This event changed Hannah completely," Nicole said. She recalled that her daughter was already fairly reserved. But after the school shooting, she became introverted and withdrew from the world.

The family got Hannah professional help for a few months after the shooting. They attended all of the trauma-healing events that the school district offered. While Hannah seemed to be recovering, all of her peers seemed to be falling apart. Nicole thought this meant Hannah was in a good place. What she came to realize later was that Hannah wasn't processing her anxiety and trauma. While the other kids were a mess, at least they were actually emoting. Hannah was putting on a brave face.

"We mistook this for doing well," Nicole recalls.

Months later, it was apparent that Hannah was struggling. She wasn't sleeping, and she had not returned to being her relaxed self. From that point forward, Nicole made sure that Hannah was involved in some type of counseling to help her heal.

CAREGIVER'S STRUGGLE

Around this same time, Nicole's father died. It seemed like everything was happening to her at once, and she wasn't allowed to fall apart. She had people depending on her. Instead, she moved from one tragic event to the next, putting out fires and holding hands. Her child's well-being would always come before her own.

Several years later, Nicole's youngest daughter, Lucy (Hannah's sister), was also impacted by gun violence. Her ex-boyfriend shot and killed a student at his school. Their family was once again rocked. Lucy took the news badly. Nicole and her family had known this young boy for many years, and she recalls feeling really confused. How could he do this? It made no sense.

Nicole will admit now that she has probably lived in a state of fight or flight since that first shooting in 2013. She suspects she has functioned with adrenal fatigue ever since. Until we talked, she didn't realize that she, too, could benefit from counseling.

At the time of my interview with Nicole (ten years after the shooting), she still reported feelings of guilt that she should have done some things differently to help Hannah. She admits feeling a sense of helplessness. School was supposed to be a safe space for her child. Yet, every day, she had to send Hannah back to the place that traumatized her.

On the day of our interview, Nicole's school was put into lockdown again. New protocols in Colorado call for periodic drills and provide an automated system that plays a recording. "LOCKDOWN, LOCKDOWN, hide, run, and fight!" is repeated on a loop until it is deemed that there is no longer a threat. By 8:30 a.m. that morning, Nicole had scurried several small children who were still in the hallway into the nearest classroom for safety. By the time she made it to her own classroom, she found that her students had followed protocol on their own, turning off the lights, huddling in the corner, and locking the door, some of them in tears.

By the time we connected for our interview at the end of her workday, Nicole was still "coming down" from the drill. She said that with each new shooting, her phone notifications go crazy with friends who are checking in on her. But Nicole is less concerned about herself. She immediately thinks about Hannah and wonders how she is coping. Each new event is a trigger from a trauma neither will ever forget.

Taylor – Ripple Effect Survivor of Gun Violence

Taylor has been a political reporter since 2019, most recently working for a local news station in Austin, Texas. It's a high-stress job. When lawmakers are in session, she spends her days at the Capitol, hustling to committee hearings and watching lengthy debates on the floor. On May 24, 2022 — the day of the Robb Elementary School shooting in Uvalde, Texas — Taylor was set to cover a runoff election in a hotly contested race for attorney general.

On that Tuesday, Taylor started her workday feeling mentally and physically prepared to cover what was on her agenda. She remembers a late start that day since she was working the night shift for the late evening news-casts. She even remembers the pantsuit that she had picked out for the election coverage. That's when she first saw chatter online about a possible active shooter situation in Uvalde. "Uvalde? Where is that?" Taylor thought. Information continued to trickle in, and around 2 p.m., there was word of reported fatalities.

BREAKING NEWS

Taylor's workday took an immediate turn. She recalls, "My colleague and I rushed out the door, packed our car with camera gear, and embarked on the three-hour drive south. We didn't really have any direction, but that is common in breaking news situations. All we knew was that we had to get there ASAP and just start trying to gather as much information as we could."

Taylor remembers how "the first few days of report-ing in Uvalde blurred together. It was like one long, trau-matic event." She felt somewhat uneasy about being part of the media onslaught in this small, intimate town. It seemed as though everyone was trying to get a sound bite. She was uncomfortable with the inhumane message this behavior sent yet was torn because she understood the importance of reporting on this mass shooting.

She interviewed the grandfather of one of the young victims. He talked about his grandson's love of baseball and pulled his wallet out to show Taylor his grandson's photo. She's never forgotten that interaction.

"When I got to my crappy motel that night, I crashed and burned. I sobbed uncontrollably in my room until my eyes were so swollen they felt heavy and tired, and I fell asleep." She continued, "The next few days, I was in a state of hypervigilance. My heart rate was high. I was on edge and felt physically nauseous having to field interviews with people who were processing unimaginable grief." Taylor went on to recount feeling sick to her stomach, not having an appetite, and feeling excessively angry and irritable. She was attempting to process shock while continuing to function well enough to get her job done.

AFTERSHOCK

Even more psychologically challenging for Taylor were the weeks and months that followed the mass shooting. Daily reports on Uvalde continued for most of the year. There were several investigations into how the Uvalde response was handled by local authorities. Because of this, there were weekly news conferences, many of which Taylor attended. Hearing families testify was a recurring reminder for her of how devastated these families were. Watching the waves of anguish unfold in front of her from week to week, she was reminded again and again of their pain and mourning.

As time passed, investigative reports were released, describing the scene in even greater detail. Taylor was exposed to images that would be unfathomable to most. These were the images she could not erase from her memory. Being on-scene the day of the event and now hearing additional descriptive details made it easy for Taylor's mind to transport itself back to the moment the shooting occurred. Eventually, she sought professional help to gain control over these excruciating images.

First Responders – Secondary Survivors of Gun Violence

More and more, we are hearing about the impacts of secondary trauma on first responders. They are often the first to arrive on the scene. It's the fire, police, and medical agencies that respond to an injury, accident, or shooting. Emergency room doctors and nurses are also part of this group and are sometimes the first people a victim remembers after a near-death experience.

These professionals need to possess extreme concentration and remain calm to do their life-saving work. But how do they handle the constant daily trauma? Where do they store the images? The smells? The moaning, screaming, and audible noises associated with a trauma scene? Yes, they are trained to remain absolutely controlled and focused on the immediate need set before them. However, they are human. They may be heroes, but their brains have the same general structure as both yours and mine, meaning that the incredibly stressful work they perform on a daily basis has an impact on their mental health.

While not a first responder, Taylor struggled with similar traumatic experiences but without the coping skills or training that first responders receive. She was one of the first to arrive at Uvalde. She was exposed to the immediate reactions of families and the community. She stored away the images and sounds of that horrible day. But this was not part of her daily routine like it would be for a trained responder. She didn't have the same skills that an EMT or firefighter would have. Taylor felt out of place and out of sorts.

Consider other jobs that lack the training to handle traumatic gun-related events. For example, think about the cleaning crews that come to a home after a horrific event, like a murder or suicide. Remember the apartment maintenance worker we talked about earlier? We might not immediately think these individuals would be affected by secondary trauma, but I know from experience that they can be. I would also suggest that this expanded population of secondary survivors is often forgotten or unrecognized when it comes to acknowledging those impacted by trauma.

A THOUGHT SPECIFICALLY FOR FIRST RESPONDERS

I know that you, too, have been exposed to horrific images, sounds, and smells. You have had to push yourselves to the limit to help save others. You have made life better for so many others by dedicating yourself to this incredible work.

Your extraordinary skills often include coping mechanisms that others do not possess. More than likely, you have the ability to find humor in these moments. You have the incredible capacity to compartmentalize. While dealing with horrible events, you can talk about the score from last night's football game or what leftovers are waiting for you in the fridge when you get home. These are skills that keep you functioning.

Many of you have had consistent exposure to unfathomable things, and you rely on this type of coping to keep you sane. I get that. However, I ask you to remember that most of us don't have these coping skills. Please keep that in mind when interacting with the survivors, family members, or bystanders who are new to the traumas they are experiencing.

I've worked as a first responder myself, responding to the scene of suicides for many years, and I completely understand the need to detach. I only suggest that you try to be aware of the family and friends of victims who are around and within earshot. I have spent many a therapy session attempting to repair the hurt experienced by family members after an interaction with a police detective, fire captain, or other emergency personnel. It is incredible how one brief interaction can be etched into their trauma story for years to come.

I recently heard a first responder say, "I've come to realize that my every day at work is the worst day in life for the people I am helping." That pretty much sums it up and is a vitally important thing to remember.

A Final Note

While perhaps difficult to read, the stories shared above are important. Each individual has experienced trauma specific to them. Their stories may be different, but they have something in common — they are all survivors.

Their stories will be revisited in the pages that follow, providing examples that will help you learn how to begin to recover from gun violence or support others who have been impacted.

Hopefully, you will begin to see that there can be a joyful life on the other side of an event that feels like overwhelming darkness.

Mental Health Professionals

What you've read in this chapter is just a small sampling of gun violence trauma. Some of you may have experienced gun violence yourselves. I suspect many have not. Regardless, for all of us in this field, gun violence survivors are a population that we can expect to see more of. With gun violence rates increasing, including child deaths, we can expect that the need for trained professionals will also be on the rise.

I implore you to learn what makes gun violence experiences different, and reading this book is a great start. This is a population that we need to become familiar with and comfortable with. I have learned through my work with survivors of suicide that they often feel misunderstood or alone. Their experiences with mental health professionals have not always been positive because those professionals have lumped their experiences into other forms of grief (for example, death by natural causes).

When it comes to gun violence, suicide loss, or other traumatic sudden losses, comparison is the enemy. Read that again. Comparison is the enemy. These clients want to feel heard and understood. They don't want their experience to be diluted because we've combined their experience into a "traditional grief" category.

If that is what you do, you will alienate that client, and that client will not return. If you do not have a comprehensive understanding of gun violence clients, you will not be a "safe space" for them. Providing well-thought-out, intentional postvention to trauma survivors can produce incredible healing and facilitate a productive, healthy life after gun violence and sudden traumatic loss.

Use the pages ahead to orient yourself on best practices for this population. I write these pages for both you and the survivors. I know that as mental health professionals, we can always benefit from a greater understanding of our clients' experiences. Thank you for trusting me and my knowledge to help expand your mindset. This willingness to learn is what will make you extraordinary in your work.

chapter 3

It Affects Everyone

Safety is not the absence of threat;
it is the presence of connection.

—GABOR MATE

I feel like the survivors' stories shared in the previous chapter are like looking at gun violence through a magnifying glass — capturing specific details and emotions in high resolution. Seeing with such clarity, hopefully, helps us better understand and have empathy for each survivor's experience and struggles.

Using these stories as a foundation, we're now going to zoom out and consider the big-picture impact of gun violence. From this perspective, it's clear that, as individuals and communities, we are suffering. Scroll through your news feed or turn on the television. Gun violence and gun tragedies have become a part of our daily lives. Just following current events exposes us to a constant barrage of gun-related tragedies, which inevitably causes stress.

This chapter will spend some time reflecting on what's happening in society. Feeling less safe in the world impacts everyone, but especially gun violence and trauma survivors. The pages that follow will explore initial reactions to trauma I've seen in clients. By taking a close look at these common reactions, you'll see the types of responses other survivors experience and know that you're not alone.

Finally, I'll begin to talk about healing. I say "begin" because I talk about it in different ways throughout the book. I've learned that it's helpful to approach healing from multiple perspectives and by using different techniques. This gives survivors the opportunity to find different strategies that work for them as they progress on their own unique healing journey.

Gun Violence Affects All of Us

Columbine High School was the first mass shooting I can recall being exposed to. It felt so big, so shocking, and so out of the ordinary. Kids were just doing what they were supposed to be doing — going to school. Schools were supposed to be safe. How could this happen?

Since that event in 1999, hearing about a mall shooting, a movie theater shooting, or another school shooting is no longer out of the ordinary. In fact, it's become almost too ordinary. It's common to get a notification on your phone or turn on the television and see the latest news story about innocent bystanders being threatened while working or even grocery shopping.

Some would say that the massive number of gun tragedies post-Columbine has desensitized us to news about mass shooting events. Yet, in a 2019 American Psychological Association poll, nearly 80 percent of American adults reported experiencing stress as a result of the possibility of a mass shooting.[7]

It seems we're both desensitized and afraid. Many adults have changed their behaviors due to this fear. They socialize differently, shop in different areas, and maybe only venture out during the daytime. For some, this fear prevents them from going to certain places or participating in events at all.

TEENS AND ESCAPE ROUTES

I can report that, in my office, I have seen firsthand the impact this fear of gun violence has had on the teenage clients I work with. During the first few weeks of the school year, the rate of anxiety in my high school clients increases. Of course, a number of things may contribute to this spike, including new environments, figuring out where you fit in socially, and getting to know new instructors and their expectations.

However, in the last several years, my teenage clients have also detailed a new stressor. *Time and time again, they have shared with me that during the first few weeks of school, they spent some time in each class period scouting out the best exit in the event of a shooting.*

My teenage clients explain how this is an almost involuntary behavior. They may not even recognize that they are doing it because it has become second nature to always look for an escape route. And this fear isn't exclusive to a school setting. Teens also report being hyperaware in other environments. When at movie theaters or concert venues, teens consciously or unconsciously scan the area and keep in mind which direction to run in case there is a shooting.

ALWAYS ON ALERT

For many, gun violence preparedness has become a part of our daily mental processing — often in subtle ways. Maybe we avoid an individual we feel is "acting strangely" because we can't be sure that person won't "shoot the place up." Maybe we fear aggravating someone while driving because that individual could have a gun in the car.

These are fears that no one was concerned with thirty years ago. However, most of us have now been exposed to gun violence, either through firsthand experience or secondhand stories. And the media provides daily updates on gun violence throughout the country.

Twenty-five years after Columbine, schools now routinely hold lockdown drills. You probably know a student who has experienced these exercises where they practice what to do in the event of an active shooter. While meant to prepare students, these sorts of drills can actually be a trigger that leaves them feeling even less safe and more anxious.[8]

These are examples of the anticipatory fear that many of us now experience. It's a new reality that our culture lives with as a result of the seemingly endless stream of gun violence events.

This combination of factors has altered the way we view the world and has caused many of us to change our behaviors in response to this perceived threat. *Exposure to gun violence has changed our perspective in one universal way — we all feel less safe.*

When It Affects You Personally

We're pulling out the magnifying glass again. The threat of gun violence adds stress to everyone's daily lives, but it especially impacts gun violence survivors. They've lived it before, so each new occurrence can be a painful reminder of their trauma.

How the brain processes trauma is interesting. There are many assumptions made about *how* someone should respond to trauma. When outsiders observe a survivor, they often suggest what that individual *should* be feeling and judge their behaviors. "How can he be going to work so soon? Obviously, he's unbothered." Or, "I can't imagine why she didn't cancel her trip. Doesn't she know that her family needs her here?" It's important not to judge the decisions others make after a traumatic event. We can't begin to understand how their brain is processing.

While each person has their own unique response to trauma, there are similarities as well. These are common first reactions I've frequently witnessed while working with gun violence survivors. Together, we navigate the following initial feelings:

- Shock and denial about the event
- Something I call "Swiss cheese brain" (or an inability to focus)
- Fear of future traumatic events

SHOCK AND DENIAL

The first thing I typically notice in individuals who have recently been traumatized is that for weeks or even months after a trauma, their brains function in a state of shock and denial. Simply put, our brains were created to protect us. Keeping us safe is the brain's primary function — more important than learning and thinking.

Think of it this way. The information from a trauma is often too colossal for the brain to process. In order to protect you, the brain decides to detach from some of its reality (the details of your trauma). In an attempt to keep you safe and to avoid a complete breakdown, your brain only processes small doses of trauma at a time.

To outsiders, this may make it appear as if you don't understand the severity of what has just occurred. It may seem odd to people that you return to work or school two days later. But in reality, what's happening is that your brain is falling back on what it knows how to do. In some ways, it is frozen, reverting to autopilot and returning to behaviors that were rote or common for you prior to the trauma. You are more comfortable in your old routine.

For some, this shock and denial may appear in strong emotional waves. One minute, there are feelings of deep despair and an inability to physically move any limbs or control tears. The next moment, they are able to hold a conversation with a neighbor about the cat they found in their backyard.

During this phase, your brain will give you one drop of information or a memory, then quickly retreat, holding back other painful details until it feels you can handle them. Often, you will function this way for quite some time, with an ebb and flow of intensity. It may look like insanity to those watching from the sidelines — one minute, you are fine, and the next, you can barely speak. I assure you, this is normal.

Just because I am using the term "denial" does not imply that you aren't fully aware that a horrific event has occurred. You absolutely are. However, your brain does not allow you to sit in that anguish and fear for long periods of time. Remember, your brain is trying to protect you by dispensing these memories in small doses. As I say to many of my clients, "This is your brain's way of keeping you out of a straitjacket or the ER."

The waves of emotion will continue for some time; however, they will become fewer and further in between.

SWISS CHEESE BRAIN

I know it's not a very technical term, but I want you to visualize what's happening. A traumatized brain is not fully functioning. Yet, for some reason, we expect it to perform as it always has. In reality, your brain may feel like it is riddled with holes. For the first year after a life-altering traumatic event, it's very common to be forgetful, mentally fatigued, or just feel a little bit like you are losing your marbles. I call this Swiss cheese brain. It can be frustrating, but there is a reason for it.

Processing a life-altering event takes energy. Grieving takes energy. I equate it to running a marathon every day. When you run a marathon, not only are your muscles taxed, but your brain is also fully engaged. Throughout

53

the race, your brain is sending you messages to keep going. It is reminding you that although you are tired, you have worked hard to prepare for this moment. It's computing how many more miles are left and trying to assess if you have enough energy left in the tank. It is processing turns, watching where the street meets the curbs. It's coaxing the feet to lift off of the ground far enough that you won't stumble.

Your brain is the ultimate cheerleader (and enemy at times), and that cheerleader gets tired. In the life of a trauma survivor, instead of sending messages to push harder to reach that next mile, your cheerleader is cheering you on to get out of bed, get dressed, or talk to a family member about the legal paperwork that needs to be completed. What about food? You will need food today. Does that mean that you will actually have to face the coworker who is going to drop by with lasagna? Will there be small talk that you just don't think you can bear? The enemy (your negative inner narrative) may be begging you to stay in bed and engage in unhealthy behaviors. So, the cheerleader will have to work even harder and be more persistent. The cheerleader, again, is getting tired!

And tomorrow, you will just have to do it all over again — only the energy will be a little more depleted than the day before. *It's a cycle that will repeat itself for some time. And it's what causes Swiss cheese brain — the brain fog that can result in the inability to recall simple things like names, dates, or where you left your car keys last night.*

What this may also look like with my clients is getting lost on their way home from work — on the route that they've driven for ten years. Or it may be walking out of the office at the end of the workday only to realize that they've left the driver's side car door wide open for eight hours, and now the battery is dead. It can also be forgetting birthdays and phone numbers, or maybe forgetting what day of the week it is and missing a child's school performance.

All these situations are common with trauma. They shouldn't be judged. You aren't broken — your brain is just running a daily marathon trying to keep you alive. So, the little things may slip.

FEAR

A gun violence survivor has just been victimized in a way they never thought would happen. I would argue that even if you live in daily fear of gun violence, you are never prepared to be a victim of it. You have completely lost trust in the world you thought you knew. You fear that it could happen again, which puts you in a state of hypervigilance.

Remember Jennifer, who was shot while out with her fiancé David? In her interview with me, she recounted years of worrying that the assailants would come back for the "kill shot." Since the perpetrators were never caught, this fear was something she had to learn to live with. As part of that fear, Jennifer shared that for years after the shooting, she would close up the house tightly at night. Every door, window, and curtain was drawn. She was obsessive about it. There wasn't an inch of daylight coming into her home, and there wasn't a sliver of glass that would expose her to the outside. An outside that had proven to be almost deadly for her on the night of her attack. It was what she had to do to make herself feel somewhat safe and secure during the hours she attempted to sleep. Could Jennifer ever feel safe again?

In the weeks, months, or even years after a traumatic event, you may be waiting for "the other shoe to drop." Anticipating that something else horrible is waiting for you around each corner. This fear can feel real, and it can be constant.

You might go about your day waiting for a phone call that a loved one was in a car accident or that another family member has taken their life. These worries are not unusual. Before your own traumatic event, those intrusive thoughts might never have crossed your mind, particularly not on a daily basis. After all, you never thought you could be a victim or so close to a traumatic event.

However, now, it may be difficult to feel any level of safety. You are grieving the loss of trust in your world. It's unsettling, and it will be uncomfortable for a while. Give it time.

You can't control what has occurred, but you can control how you process it. The goal is to regain control.

Healing

Gun violence has become woven into our society. It's a powerful stressor for everyone. Knowing this stress exists gives us an understanding that healing needs to happen on both an individual and community level.

Gun violence survivors, in particular, need specific tools and support to heal from their trauma. By explaining how initial reactions to trauma are similar, I hope survivors become more aware of what they're feeling and will realize they are not alone. It's important to understand *what* is happening internally, and then we can discuss *how* to correct it.

Here are a few other things I always suggest:

Be gentle with yourself or your loved one. Be patient. Remind yourself that some of your reactions are a response to trauma and that your brain is attempting to protect you.

Don't have expectations. There is no linear way to process this. It is just that — a process. And it's not anyone else's process. It is uniquely yours. So don't feel the need to meet others' expectations either.

Avoid big decisions. This is probably not the time for big changes. Being in a state of shock and denial does not typically lead to the clearest thinking and decision-making. There will be time for that later.

Shift your focus to unremarkable things. Take note of the days when nothing out of the ordinary happens. Odds are that there will be many more quiet days than ones where something goes wrong.

Slowly, with time, things will begin to feel more normal. Healing is possible. Most importantly, cut yourself some slack as you process trauma. It's a big deal, and you're doing big work.

fast facts

▸ A majority of American adults report feeling stressed about the possibility of a mass shooting.

▸ Shock and denial are typical psychological responses to trauma. This is the brain's way of protecting a survivor.

▸ Processing a life-altering event takes energy. The energy that is stolen from the brain may result in forgetfulness and mental fatigue. I have named this slowed-down functioning as Swiss cheese brain.

▸ It's not uncommon for a trauma survivor to live in a state of hypervigilance, living in fear that another catastrophic event may occur.

Mental Health Professionals

Many Americans are stressed by the prevalence of gun-related violence and the possibility of mass shootings. Keep this stressor in mind. It may impact a range of clients. In addition to direct victims, you may be treating several secondary survivors, first responders, or ripple effect survivors. These individuals have also experienced trauma.

Expect a new trauma survivor to exhibit signs of shock and denial for some period of time. Normalize this experience for them. These clients will need your assurance that they are not "broken" and that their mental faculties will return in time. It helps the healing process if your client has a greater understanding of why they feel how they feel. Mental fatigue, loss of emotional control, and brain fog are normal reactions to trauma.

Explain how the brain is trying to protect the survivor and simultaneously heal itself. These efforts take a great deal of energy, and your client may not realize how draining this can be. The brain's effort to heal requires an expenditure of energy that can create emotional and physical fatigue for months. Helping clients understand the mechanics of the brain's response to trauma will help calm the survivor and normalize their experience.

Also, teach your clients ways to give themselves grace and help them embrace this phase of healing. This trauma has impacted the survivor's confidence. On top of feeling fatigued, they may doubt their abilities. Sometimes, accomplishing the bare minimum of daily tasks is enough for now. Teach them to go easy on themselves. And remind them that, in time, they will regain clarity and energy.

Encourage secondary survivors to seek their own support. This quiet group needs to be seen. They need to be told that their belief that they "don't have it as bad as someone else" or "should know better than anyone how to take care of themselves" is simply not true. These individuals need and will benefit from support that will help them release their traumatic experiences. This is particularly true for mental health providers and first responders who are continually supporting other trauma victims.

the

Mechanics

of

Trauma

Chapter 4

Trauma and the Brain

The road to freedom is always filled with roadblocks.
Comfort is staying in what you know and
what isn't working just because it's certain.

—ANONYMOUS

In order to begin the healing process, it is helpful to have an understanding of how your brain and body process trauma. You may find that some of what you read in the upcoming chapters is familiar to you. You might have experienced particular symptoms firsthand yet didn't quite know the source of your discomfort. *By learning about what's happening to you physically, you will be better prepared to recognize and understand why you feel the way you do.*

The following pages are filled with a lot of information. Take it slowly or skim if needed. Maybe you'll want to go back and read it a second time — whatever works best for you.

The main objective of this chapter is to give you a better understanding of how your brain has changed after trauma.

Put simply, the brain's primary job is to protect you. It is hardwired to make decisions that will keep you alive and functioning. The brain automatically keeps you breathing. It reminds you that you need nutrients by signaling stomach pangs, and it causes your mouth to be dry when you need to hydrate. When a threat or danger is perceived, it shifts into survival mode, giving you additional alertness and adrenaline to respond.

After a traumatic event, the brain's need to protect itself can activate a long-term survival mode that keeps you in a state of constant vigilance, resulting in fatigue, a lack of focus, and feeling overwhelmed. It's important to understand this response to trauma so you can learn to react in an effective way.

In this chapter, we're going to take a deep dive into the brain and how it functions. You'll learn how the brain behaves when it's under stress and how to identify this response in yourself. The more you are able to make sense of how trauma is impacting you, the better equipped you will be to find ways to provide calm for yourself. By understanding what is happening to you after a trauma, you'll be able to regain some of the control you feel you have lost as a result of this event.

Survival Mode

Patty came in to see me after losing her college-age son to a sudden death. His death was an utter shock to her.

As a mom of two other surviving children, Patty's primary concern was for their well-being. What started out as compassionate concern for her surviving boys quickly turned to obsessive worry. Will one of them turn to drugs in their grief? Were they being mistreated by their friends? Could another tragic event occur?

These concerns didn't pass over time. Instead, they grew, becoming more elaborate and more frequent. Patty had become singularly focused on her surviving children and keeping them safe, even though it didn't appear that they were at increased risk of harm. Patty was waiting for the other shoe to drop — she was functioning in survival mode.

We know the brain works hard to protect us. When facing a threat, it puts us into a response mode that takes over during a time of incredible stress. This survival mode shuts down all nonessential body and mind functions, and every ounce of energy is put into preparing the body for its best survival response. In Patty's case, she was determined to assure her children's survival above all else. That was a part of her process.

For some, *even after the immediate threat ceases, the body and mind can remain in a state of constant survival mode.* This perpetual state of alertness prepares us to be ready to respond to any challenge or threat (a.k.a., waiting for that other shoe to drop). These threats may be perceived or real; the brain can't differentiate.

Remaining in this long-term state of heightened alertness increases the risk of depression, anxiety, and substance use. Additionally, this stress on the body increases the risk of cancer, heart disease, chronic disease, and chronic pain. It may even shorten life span.[9]

FIGHT, FLIGHT, FREEZE, AND FAWN

You may already be familiar with the four main responses to threatening situations — *fight, flight, freeze, and fawn.* Let's discuss what those terms really mean and how they show up in response to trauma. Remember, these responses can occur during a traumatic event, after a traumatic event has passed, or in response to *what is perceived* to be a threatening situation. Some of these reactions may be experienced for months after a trauma has occurred.

Fight – In this mode, the brain tries to fight or defend against a threat. This might result in:

- Engaging in verbal or physical altercations
- Having feelings of intense anger
- Controlling and/or bullying others

Flight – When in flight mode, the brain has an overwhelming desire to escape or deny pain or emotional distress. This could appear as follows:

- Using work or studies as an excuse not to engage in certain areas of your life
- Ending a relationship when you feel threatened before the other person can break up with you
- Using work, hobbies, or even alcohol and substances to avoid feelings of fear, anxiety, or panic

Freeze – The brain uses freeze mode as a stall tactic while it decides whether it's better to fight or flee. The following may result:

- Preferring solitude and avoiding close relationships
- Detaching physically from the world through sleep or by staying in your room or house
- Mentally "checking out" from situations you feel could be stressful or painful (this could be almost anything at first)

Fawn – When in fawn mode, the brain feels the need to please people it fears may be a danger. Fawn behavior includes:

- Agreeing to whatever your partner asks of you, even if you'd rather not
- Constantly praising a manager in hopes of avoiding criticism or negative feedback
- Having few boundaries around your own needs

TRAUMA RESPONSES

Fight
- Explosive Outbursts
- Controlling
- Bullying
- Behaving aggressively
- Demanding perfection from others

Freeze
- Isolating self from others
- Spacing out / Feeling numb
- Having difficulty making decisions
- Disassociating
- Being a couch potato

Flight
- Rushing around / Difficulty sitting still
- Striving to be perfect
- Using work as an escape
- Feelings of panic or anxiety
- Over-thinking / Obsessive thinking

Fawn
- Struggling to say no to others
- Avoiding conflict
- Co-Dependency
- Having limited or no boundaries
- People-pleasing

How Trauma Changes the Brain

Just like chronic stress, trauma can alter your brain, making it a challenge to accomplish all of the daily tasks that you were able to complete with ease prior to the event. Attempting to be productive can be a real test. If you are feeling this, you are not alone.

In the aftermath of trauma, one of the most difficult aspects for survivors is understanding the changes that are occurring in their brains and bodies. Trauma survivors are aware that they feel different. But they often can't put their finger on why their memory is foggy or why they are always anxious or jumpy.

TRAUMA AND BRAIN FUNCTION

According to scientific research, following a traumatic event, your brain goes through physiological changes that would not have occurred if there had been no trauma. Yes — your brain looks and functions differently after trauma. In fact, if we performed a brain scan before and after, we would see the changes. You aren't imagining it!

Sometimes, the discomfort caused by trauma gets integrated into our worldview quickly, resolving the stress. In other instances, the physiological changes make it hard, if not impossible, to function, interfering with relationships, work, and daily activities.

If you notice these changes occurring, take the time to step back and assess. How have your relationships changed? Can you focus at work or complete everyday tasks? Do you feel easily fatigued, even when you haven't exerted much energy?

Researchers have identified three major areas of the brain that are impacted following trauma.[10] The physiological changes in these areas result in imbalances that impact recovery and healing. Trauma and your response to it can create faulty wiring in the brain. Fortunately, gaining an understanding of how these brain functions impact us can give us information and tools to heal and recover.

What follows is a mini biology lesson. Don't get bogged down with remembering terms and functions. The goal is to give you a general explanation of what's going on in your brain so you understand the changes that are occurring and can get the right help to continue healing.

OVERSTIMULATED AMYGDALA

The amygdala is a small, almond-shaped part of the brain that has a big job. It serves as the major processing center for your emotions. It stores memories and connects them with your emotions. It also activates the fight-or-flight response. While this is essential for survival when facing imminent danger, *after a trauma, the amygdala can get caught in a state of habitual high alert.* When overstimulated in this way, it can create a repeating loop of perceived threats everywhere and all the time.

UNDERACTIVE HIPPOCAMPUS

The main function of the hippocampus involves learning, storing new memories, and regulating emotions.

One of its biggest jobs is to take our short-term memories and shift them into our long-term memory. After a trauma, the increased stress hormones can kill certain cells in the hippocampus, making it less effective. This simple interruption in the process keeps the body and brain stimulated in a reactive mode. *Your brain never gets the message that the threat has passed, so it stays in a continuous state of preparing for the perceived threat.*

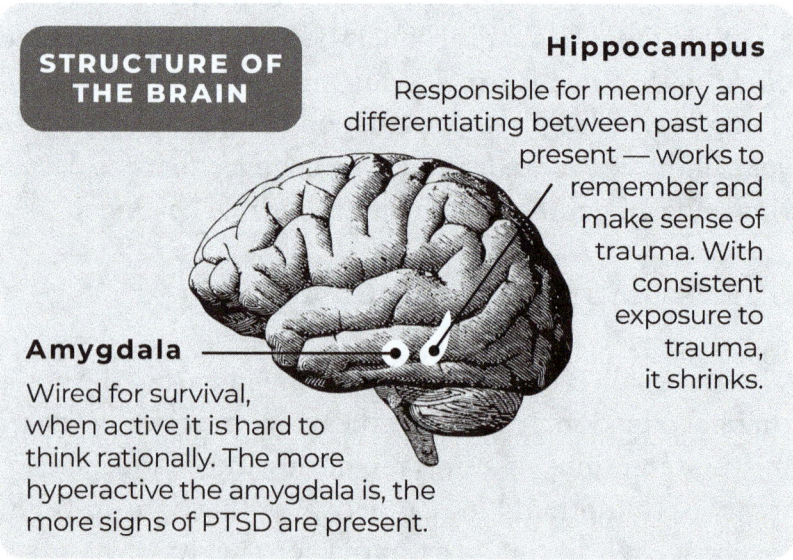

STRUCTURE OF THE BRAIN

Hippocampus
Responsible for memory and differentiating between past and present — works to remember and make sense of trauma. With consistent exposure to trauma, it shrinks.

Amygdala
Wired for survival, when active it is hard to think rationally. The more hyperactive the amygdala is, the more signs of PTSD are present.

ELEVATED STRESS LEVELS

Continually elevated stress hormones disrupt the body's ability to regulate or calm itself. *Being constantly on alert keeps you overactivated, which leads to incredible fatigue of the body and mind.* It's exhausting!

Understanding these brain changes can help us to make sense of some of the physical responses and brain fog we may be experiencing. These simple changes pack a big punch in disrupting our everyday lives.

They are all normal ways that trauma can show up in the brain. The good news is that these effects can be temporary. Your brain function can return to what it was prior to your trauma. The amygdala can learn to relax, and the hippocampus can return to proper functioning. Like any injury or illness, it just takes time and the proper treatment to heal.

Recognizing what is happening will create a different inner narrative about your healing. With understanding comes control, *and regaining control over your trauma is really what this book is about.*

▸ You are not imagining it if you feel "off" or different.

▸ Trauma physiologically changes the way your brain functions. Images of a brain before and after a traumatic event show distinct differences in the brain.

▸ You may feel less in control of your emotions and be frustrated that you can't recall memories.

▸ You may feel like you're in a constant state of alert, which can trigger the fight, flight, freeze, or fawn response.

▸ Completing simple tasks may feel exhausting and "extra" for you. You are easily fatigued both physically and mentally.

▸ Understanding what's going on in your brain can help you regain control and heal.

Mental Health Professionals

The work of helping the brain heal is complicated. You need to be present with your client. In the first few months of this relationship, focus less on your treatment plan and more on supporting your clients' emotions and normalizing their experiences. I have found that educating trauma victims about what is going on in their brains and bodies is a powerful way of supporting them. Without this understanding, survivors often feel as if they are "going crazy" or are "permanently broken." If they don't understand why the body is reacting in the way that it is, they may start to believe that the damage is irrevocable.

A trauma victim's sense of control has been stolen from them. By helping them understand their neurological and physical responses to trauma, you help them see that these responses are normal and that the brain's primary functions can be healed. They can begin to believe that, eventually, they will regain control, and this provides hope.

Teach your clients that what they say to themselves matters. The brain believes what you tell it. If they tell themselves that they are "forever damaged," their brains will begin to live into that narrative. It is important to help survivors choose their thoughts intentionally.

You can help them reframe their thinking so that "I am so screwed up I'll never be the same" or "I don't know who I am anymore" can become "My brain and body are responding to extreme stress. I am the same person I was before. And just like if I had a broken leg, I need to be patient and allow my brain to heal."

Chapter 5

Trauma and the Body

Very few of us had our grief, our losses held adequately by anybody. That unheld material doesn't just dissipate, doesn't just go away. It burrows in and becomes someplace that we will return to at some point.

—FRANCIS WELLER, MARRIAGE AND FAMILY THERAPIST

Trauma is a tricky thing. It impacts your mind and body, often in ways you may not even notice. Do you remember Hannah, who survived a school shooting by spending hours hiding in her high school's dark theater? Months after the event, Hannah found herself feeling triggered by small things completely unrelated to the shooting. These feelings reached a crisis level on a dark and snowy evening when she was waiting for a train that was running late.

People around her were getting worried and started talking about the delay, wondering if the train would ever come. Some were even debating what to do if they were stranded in the cold weather. As these conversations swirled around her, Hannah's body began to shake and sweat. She was physically responding to her feelings of fear, and her body was telling her that she was in danger. For Hannah, the experience took her back to the dark theater and the school shooting. She was once again hiding in the dark, trying to be small, and hoping to be rescued. Hannah was experiencing her first panic attack.

Hannah's story illustrates how trauma can have a physical impact on the body long after trauma has occurred. Even though she was physically safe at the train station, the train delay triggered her fears in a physical way. She felt out of control and afraid. When Hannah thinks back to that night, she now realizes her fear spiked because things weren't going as expected, which brought her directly back to her trauma. She began to understand that unpredictable events were difficult for her to manage and process.

Physical reactions to trauma are very common, but these troubling responses can be overcome. Part of this process involves learning how to become better in tune with your body and how it reacts in different situations. Knowing these things can help the healing process. However, *left uncared for, trauma can physically wear your body down.*

Recognizing how your body holds trauma and how this stress shows up in your muscles, organs, and joints can help you heal. Better yet, you can use this information to develop skills that will change these reactions. Now, get ready for a deep dive into the mind-body connection as we look at ways you can use this information to heal.

How the Body Holds Trauma

While I think many recognize the mental aspects of trauma, I have found that the physical impact of trauma on the body isn't always valued or understood, particularly in medical or therapeutic settings.

Many clients come to me with a variety of persistent, unexplained physical issues: sudden aches and pains, an inability to take a deep breath, or viral infections that just won't go away. These clients don't have the physical energy to seek help for these ailments, or when they do, the findings are inconclusive. Tests come back negative. Ultrasounds show no injury. The result? The physical pain becomes another stressor on top of their trauma. They feel as if they have no control over their environment and that their bodies are failing them. Talk about feeling helpless.

I help clients understand that the physical symptoms they are experiencing could be their body's reaction to trauma. I often compare the body to an orchestra — a large group of musicians who are led by a conductor. Sections of different instruments work together to create sounds and harmonies. Led by the conductor, the different sections coordinate with each other to create a single, harmonious melody. Similarly, the body contains multiple unique systems led by the brain. Each system performs a specific function and, by working together, helps the entire body function as a single entity.

When a trauma occurs, some systems may break down, which makes it difficult, if not impossible, for the entire system to operate effectively. Understanding the deep connection between the brain and body can help us better understand how trauma can impact us and how we can heal.

The Body Keeps the Score

Both research and my clients have shown me the strong relationship that exists between depression and physical symptoms, like body aches, fatigue, and changes in appetite. Someone experiencing depression may feel stiffness in their joints or even chronic pain.

I've seen this in patients and experienced it firsthand with my father. After he retired, he began having pain and discomfort — persistent shoulder pain or a shooting pain traveling down his arm or up his neck. At times, he would sigh or groan from the pain, not knowing how to make it stop. He went through a revolving door of doctors' offices, having tests, blood draws, and ultrasounds. All results were inconclusive, yet his pain was very real.

My father was depressed, and his pain was a physical manifestation of his mental discomfort. He had lost an important part of his life when he stopped working, and he was aging. Those two events are not easy for men to process. I understood his depression, but I was intrigued by how it was expressed physically in his body.

I started to read more about the mind-body connection and came upon Bessel van der Kolk's book *The Body Keeps the Score*.[11] He's a brilliant physician and researcher who has spent his career studying how children and adults adapt after experiencing traumatic events.

His research shows that being traumatized is not only an issue of being stuck in the past. It also means that we're not completely living in the present moment. Additionally, until the trauma is resolved, the stress response stays activated, and the body continues to release cortisol and other stress hormones. This heightened state of activation negatively impacts the body. Usually, after a stressful event ends, cortisol levels decrease. However, chronic stressors can keep cortisol levels high. When this goes unchecked, it wears the body down on a cellular level.[12]

This sounds like what Hannah's mom, Nicole, experienced. She admits that she has probably lived in a state of fight-or-flight since that first shooting in 2013 and suspects she has functioned with adrenal fatigue ever since. Nicole continued to function on autopilot, completing her daily tasks and pushing through the weariness, not realizing that there were things she could do to provide relief for herself. Until we talked during the interview for this book, Nicole didn't realize that she, too, could benefit from counseling.

To heal from the past, survivors need to be aware of their bodies and their reactions in order to help them disconnect or unlearn chronic fight-or-flight mode.

UNADDRESSED TRAUMA

This was not a concept we learned when I was in graduate school. So, until I read van der Kolk's book, I didn't fully comprehend the importance of how trauma could impact your body in ways that are even greater than the aches and pains brought on by depression. Observing that many of my clients shared this similarity of illness and/or physical pain after experiencing a life-altering or traumatic event led me to dig even deeper.

What I found was an extensive collection of trauma-related research that recognized how unaddressed trauma can be a contributing factor to many illnesses. It is associated with eight of the ten leading causes of death, including diabetes, heart conditions, strokes, lung and kidney disease, cancer, suicide, and accidental overdose.

Unless this trauma is addressed, prevention and treatment can be less effective and, in some cases, not effective at all. That is powerful information, and I don't believe it is given the neon-sign emphasis that it deserves in the medical and mental health space.

What I want you to understand is that unresolved trauma can fire up the brain's stress response system, which, in turn, impacts your body's joints, organs, and muscles. When a traumatic event makes us feel out of control, it helps to realize that we can do something about our body's reaction. We can regain control.

POST-TRAUMATIC STRESS DISORDER (PTSD)

Post-traumatic stress disorder (PTSD) has become almost a casual catchphrase to exaggerate how a situation was stressful. "Walking past that restaurant gave me PTSD. Do you remember how sick I was the last time I ate there?" It's a term we've gotten used to throwing into the middle of a story to give it emphasis. I've included information here on PTSD because so many trauma survivors ask about the symptoms associated, wondering if some of what they are experiencing falls under this category.

For gun violence and trauma survivors, PTSD can be a serious issue. The symptoms commonly experienced can impact both the body and the mind. These symptoms can occur after either experiencing or witnessing a traumatic event. Someone suffering from PTSD experiences extreme distress, and their daily lives and relationships are disrupted. Rather than feeling a little better each day, symptoms don't go away and interfere with normal life.

In addition, people who have experienced childhood trauma or suffered from PTSD are ten times more likely to experience chronic pain due to the mind-body connection.[13] Are you beginning to see how powerful this connection is?

There are a variety of ways PTSD presents itself, and it's often not clear if a survivor's struggles should be categorized as PTSD. To provide some clarity, I have listed four general categories of PTSD symptoms. Each category can vary in severity:

- **Intrusive thoughts:** Recurrent memories of the trauma, nightmares, or flashbacks
- **Changes in mood:** Negative thoughts about self and others, emotional numbness, difficulty maintaining relationships, feelings of hopelessness
- **Hypervigilance:** Easily startled, trouble sleeping or concentrating, always on guard for danger, feelings of guilt, and/or irritability
- **Avoidance:** Avoids thinking about their trauma and/or avoids people, places, or activities that remind them of the event[14]

Physical symptoms may be expressed as unexpected rage or tears, increased heart rate, shortness of breath, shaking, nightmares, insomnia, loss of appetite, or emotional numbness. Additionally, memory loss and difficulty concentrating often occur.

Individuals with post-traumatic stress disorder (PTSD) experience a natural stress response to a traumatic event. *They can feel confused and struggle to understand how their minds and bodies are suddenly so out of control.* Researcher Michele Rosenthal explains, "The problem isn't that the survivor won't 'just get over it,' but that she needs time, help, and the opportunity to discover her own path to healing in order to do so."[15]

If you feel that these symptoms sound like what you're experiencing, you may want to consider seeking a formal assessment with a mental health professional.

PTSD FACTS

- Six out of every 100 people will experience PTSD at some point in their lives.
- 15.4 percent of shooting and stabbing victims develop PTSD.
- 14.3 percent of people who suddenly and unexpectedly experience the death of a close loved one develop PTSD.
- Witnessing the murder or serious injury of another person causes PTSD in 7.3 percent of people.[16]

Trauma and the Vagus Nerve

When your body perceives a threat, it is likely to react like Hannah's did on the train platform. It kicks into what I call high-alert mode, allowing the brain and body to take over to protect you. When the threat has passed and you're safe, your body shifts into calm-down mode, which helps you slow down and relax. Ideally, the two systems work together to keep the body balanced and ready to handle whatever happens.

Luckily, when we find ourselves in a prolonged state of high alert, the body has a backup system called the vagus nerve, which works to calm this alert-mode response.

Vagus is Latin for wandering, and the vagus nerve earns this name as the longest cranial nerve in the body. The vagus nerve travels from the brain stem all the way to the abdomen and interacts with nearly every organ in the body. The nerve's main purpose is to help the body return to rest and calm, especially after a stressful situation. Because it exchanges information back and forth between the body and brain, some call this nerve the information superhighway of the body.

When the vagus nerve is overstimulated because of prolonged stress, it can impact all the tissues and muscles it comes in contact with, from your neck down to your abdomen. The nerve sends negative messages back to the brain, which, in turn, creates inflammation. This type of chronic inflammation can lead to disease.

It may be hard to imagine that microscopic changes in the body have such a huge impact, but they do. Our bodies physically respond to stress in ways we were never taught or even imagined.

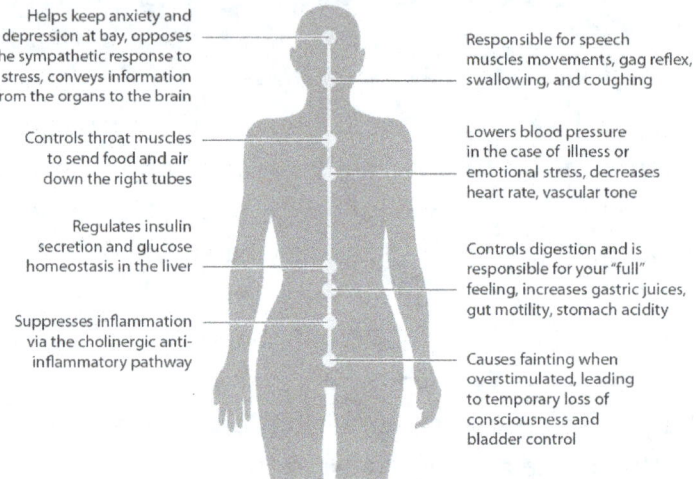

WHAT THE VAGUS NERVE DOES

Vagus nerve effects on the organ systems.

Helps keep anxiety and depression at bay, opposes the sympathetic response to stress, conveys information from the organs to the brain

Controls throat muscles to send food and air down the right tubes

Regulates insulin secretion and glucose homeostasis in the liver

Suppresses inflammation via the cholinergic anti-inflammatory pathway

Responsible for speech muscles movements, gag reflex, swallowing, and coughing

Lowers blood pressure in the case of illness or emotional stress, decreases heart rate, vascular tone

Controls digestion and is responsible for your "full" feeling, increases gastric juices, gut motility, stomach acidity

Causes fainting when overstimulated, leading to temporary loss of consciousness and bladder control

Used with permission from Ross Hauser, M.D., and Caring Medical Florida. CaringMedical.com

CALMING THE VAGUS NERVE

The good news is that calming your vagus nerve serves as a sort of override system on the high-alert and calm-down modes.

After my father died, I was trying to hold it together for myself, my clients, and my family. It was a lot to handle. I wasn't able to catch my breath, literally, and my chest felt constricted and tight. My shoulders were always tight to my ears, and I never felt relaxed.

I didn't realize it, but I was functioning in a continuous high-alert mode. My body wasn't getting any rest, and I was exhausted. A friend suggested I try a specialist in vagus nerve manipulation. I was skeptical because this was a new form of treatment for me, and it sounded a little "out there." But after one session, I experienced substantial physical relief, and I was a believer.

Tony, the specialist, explained how the vagus nerve contracts when it is stressed, which naturally shortens the rope that winds through your abdomen. With prolonged stress, this shortened vagus nerve resulted in my organs being pressed together, preventing them from being able to fully expand or perform to their full capability. No wonder I couldn't take a deep breath for months. My lungs were bunched up against my heart and other organs. Working with a specialist on the vagus nerve proved to be very helpful in reducing my physical discomfort.

A lot of research supports the important role of the vagus nerve and its response to trauma. I learned about it from a trusted source and then did some digging on my own. Most importantly, I then stepped outside my comfort zone and found the physical relief I so desperately needed. I also discovered that there were more options available than I realized to support my healing. I just had to look a little closer, ask around, and step out of my familiarity.

You Can Heal

Your body is resilient. *By understanding how the body physically responds to stress hormones and a prolonged state of high alert, you can learn what to avoid and how to manage what you can't avoid. Learning these skills puts you in charge and is the first step to reprogramming your brain and body as you move toward real healing.*

Changes to the brain due to trauma may seem disastrous and even permanent. *But I want to repeat the truth that these changes can be reversed.*

- The amygdala can learn to relax.
- The hippocampus can resume proper memory functioning.
- The nervous system can return to its easy flow between high-alert and calm-down modes.

Achieving a state of balance and healing involves conscious work to redirect the body and mind. Without this intentional work to reset and reprogram your mind, you may struggle with the following:

- Anger
- Detachment from others
- Resentment
- Victimhood
- Anxiety/fear/isolation
- Difficulty with trust

The options for reversing this damage are limitless and individual. Several methods can be used to retrain the mind so that it can reframe and release its grip on trauma. Approaches include techniques to release muscle tension, bodywork (we discussed vagus work already), and cognitive retraining. Survivors are unique, and the healing path is determined by each individual's needs and experiences. Don't be afraid to try different things until you find a therapy that works for you. The goal is to find a method to help you, so don't stop until you find it.

You are too important not to try!

fast facts

▸ The body and mind are connected. Physical reactions to trauma are very common. Learning how to become better in tune with your body and how it reacts in different situations can help the healing process.

▸ Unresolved trauma can lead to prolonged stress and physically wear your body down. It increases stress hormones, which impacts the body's joints, organs, and muscles. You aren't imagining it.

▸ Pay attention to your body's response to trauma. When an event makes you feel out of control, it helps to realize that you can regain control of your body's reaction.

▸ Your body is resilient, and you can heal. It is a conscious process. Don't be afraid to try different things until you find a therapy that works for you. The goal is to find a method to help you specifically, so don't stop until you find it.

Mental Health Professionals

If you are working in grief and trauma, learn as much as possible about how the body responds to trauma. Bessel van der Kolk's book, The Body Keeps the Score, is a must-read for anyone working in this area. If you don't explore these concepts in advance, you'll be learning along with your clients, and you won't be able to help them as efficiently. Preparing ahead of time will help to normalize clients' experiences and guide them to relief.

Reinforcing the mind-body connection with your client is important. The more they understand about what could be happening to their bodies, the more they will understand how their actions can influence and change these effects. They'll learn that they may have more control over their healing than they realize. Help them come to this revelation.

As a trained mental health professional, you should be proud of the work you do! It's hard stuff! But don't stop there; encourage your clients to be open to other modalities. Set your ego aside. Talk therapy is not the solution for all trauma survivors. Some may benefit from a combination of talk therapy and other options, including somatic bodywork, yoga, vagus nerve manipulation, or EMDR.

If you have built a strong rapport with your clients, they will trust your guidance. The more you know about these modalities, the better you can explain and represent them. Visit centers that work in somatic healing. Make phone calls. Experience these techniques yourself. After all, you are an important role model for your client.

Understanding Reactions *to* Trauma

Chapter 6

Inner Narratives

We do not see things as they are;
we see them as WE are.

—ANAÏS NIN

Our lives are filled with experiences that influence how we see the world. It could be where we grew up, how many siblings we have, or even who our best friend was in fourth grade. These experiences make us who we are and uniquely us. They shape how we interact with others, make decisions, and see the world. After trauma, the way we perceive our world is dramatically and forever changed.

Your story has shifted, and this impacts how you think about yourself and the world around you. A world that was once filled with sunshine may now be perceived as cloudy and slightly dangerous. It makes perfect sense to feel differently about yourself and the world after trauma. Everything has changed, and your go-to reactions may no longer feel natural.

To make better sense of these feelings, we're going to explore the importance of understanding your inner narrative — the stories you tell yourself. Then, we'll talk about how you can begin to slowly change unhelpful narratives to create space for healing. *You can't control what has happened, but you can control how you process it.*

Inner Narratives

An inner narrative is a story. It's your story. It's how you see the world through your own unique lens, which is a combination of your experiences, beliefs, and thoughts. Your inner narrative also influences your understanding of what's happening around you and how you process and interpret it.

On a daily basis, it's that voice you hear in your mind telling you what to believe. Sometimes, it plays messages on repeat. It could be something as simple as telling you that you can't possibly like broccoli as an adult because you didn't like it as a kid. Or it could be a much more painful thought telling you that you are forever broken after your traumatic experience. In either case, your inner narrative is not always logical or reliable. However, we do give it a lot of credit — sometimes too much.

By defining inner narrative, we're taking the first step toward managing it. It's not always telling you the truth, and it's okay to question it. In fact, it's important to question it. Why? Because your brain believes what you tell it. Just because you think a thought, that doesn't mean it's true. It's important to step back so you can observe and evaluate your thoughts, especially negative ones causing you distress.

REMEMBER:
Your brain believes what you tell it.

Your Perspective

I'm sure you've seen crime shows with lineups where people have to identify the suspected criminal. Two people who experienced the same robbery try to point out the bad guy. All too often, these witnesses choose two different individuals as the perpetrator. Maybe one of them recalls that the alleged criminal was wearing dark grey suit pants, and the other is sure he was in navy joggers. The witnesses may have experienced the same event, yet they remember it very differently, committing different details to memory. This is true for you and your trauma as well.

How you remember a traumatic event can be quite different from how someone else remembers the same event. We all create our own inner narratives made up of specific details that stood out to us in those frightening moments. These observations could be different for the person standing next to you. Experiences can vary widely.

What version of the traumatic event do you have committed to your memory? Take some time to really think about that. Have you taken your unique memories and blended them with the memories others have shared with you? Maybe a parent or your partner has suggested that you've remembered it all wrong. Maybe someone has given you some additional information that was not originally included in your version of the story. Maybe you've seen other details in the media? Have you added someone else's perspective to your personal narrative?

In my case, I was only six years old at the time of my kidnapping. My family never spoke of it again after the day it happened (at least not in my presence). I only had my own version of the story to rely on — interpreted by a six-year-old.

Generally, we tend to stick with one version of the story and commit it to memory. That version is the one that is replayed internally many times; it is the story that becomes our truth. Now, as a six-year-old child, was my memory absolutely perfect? I suspect not. But honestly, it doesn't matter if the specific details are accurate.

At six, I only had so much experience, and my mom was a focal point in my life. So, I'm not surprised that many of the lasting effects of my kidnapping were centered around fear for my mom's safety. This, after all, was *my* version of the story. No one else's. It is the version I committed to my memory, and it became my truth.

My siblings and dad have their own version of the kidnapping. They may not have been in the car with us, but I suspect my dad could never forget the phone call he received from the police or racing away from his office to come and be reunited with us.

After the police interviewed my mom and me, a patrol car was sent to our home to look for the perpetrators. My siblings have memories of a police cruiser pulling into our driveway. My brother and his friend were approached in our driveway as if they were the bad guys. That's frightening for a teenager.

My dad and siblings experienced scenarios that were complicated, but they didn't belong to me. They also did not match my narrative. Each member of my family would have to work through their own unique scenarios. I couldn't understand theirs, and they couldn't understand mine.

When you begin your healing work, take note of your inner narrative and your unique perspective. *What version of the event are you telling yourself? Try to weed out what others are telling you is true (or not true).*

In reality, it doesn't matter. All that matters is the version you have committed to your memory. That is the version you will need to heal! Be prepared to share this narrative with a professional when you are ready.

What's Your Movie Reel?

Trauma stories are often committed to memory in a form that's like a movie reel or a short video stored on your phone. When you need to access that memory, your brain simply goes to your internal camera roll, and the scene begins to play. For some survivors, this movie reel plays on repeat, even when they don't want it to.

What **version** of

the event are you

telling yourself?

Try to **weed out**

what **others** are

telling you is **true**

(or **not true**).

Even if your trauma played out over a series of minutes, hours, or days, your brain typically condenses it into a short story. It is this shortened version of the story that your mind goes back to every time you talk about or relive the event. This movie reel is part of your inner narrative. There are voices, themes, and a sequence of events that play out each time this movie is accessed.

Taylor, the reporter who responded to Uvalde to report on the mass shooting at Robb Elementary, spoke with me about her trauma and what she remembers. She recalled repeated images of children hiding under their desks, shielding themselves from the shooter. Taylor had not witnessed this happening. However, she had visited the school, knew vaguely how a classroom in Robb Elementary School was configured, and could, therefore, envision the terrified children fearing for their lives as they crouched under their desks.

This became Taylor's movie reel. As time passed, when reminded of the trauma, her mind would go to this reel and run it on a loop. Taylor needed professional help to resolve these images. Gaining better control over these movie reels gave her greater control over her trauma.

SNAPSHOTS

Interestingly, sometimes, our minds break down a movie reel into even smaller pieces. It may be that the brain shortens the movie reel in order to process the trauma in small segments. I call these snapshots. Like the movie reels, it's essential to process or understand these individual moments in order to heal.

Jennifer, who was ambushed with her fiancé, organized part of her story into snapshots. When I spoke with her about the day she was shot, she described the first part of her day as if she were reading a novel. She set up the story by telling me about her life before the shooting. As she described her daily activities before the shooting, they were fluid, one page blending and leading into the next with ease.

However, once she began sharing the moments of the shooting, her dialogue changed. She told her story frame by frame, relaying each specific moment — when the first gunshot was heard, the point where she ducked for cover, the belief that the shooters would come back to "finish her off," and the physical pain as the chest tube was inserted without any anesthesia in the emergency room. These were her own individual snapshots in time — each picture loaded with its own terror and fear.

If you have committed your trauma to memory in snapshots, you may need to heal each frame separately. This may sound overwhelming, but like dominoes, once you get started, it's a chain reaction.

THE WHAT IFS

Some people have a movie reel or snapshots, while others become preoccupied with questions. They wonder — How did this happen? How did this person get a gun? What if someone had stopped them before they could hurt me? What if we didn't go to a movie that night? What if I hadn't taken that call from my boss and had left the office on time? What if my dad had gotten my mom the help that I told him she needed? Who failed me?

These thoughts and questions create another part of your story. Your mind can be relentless when it comes to "what ifs." What if something was different? Then, the bad thing wouldn't have happened to me. What if someone did their job better? Then, that person wouldn't have been able to hurt me. *Feelings of resentment and anger are often twisted within the "what ifs."*

Can you recall any "what ifs" that you have been obsessing over since your trauma? How does your body respond to these questions when you think about them? Will finding an answer to any of these questions really bring you peace or change your future?

Take some time to examine your inner narrative. Do you have a story about your story? If you hold resentments about how someone could have handled the situation differently and changed the trajectory of your trauma, it's important to figure out how to release those feelings.

Anger and resentment won't change the events of that day. But they will delay your healing. I know that letting go can be a tall order. I don't expect it to come easily for you — especially not immediately. But just keep it in the back of your mind. Come back to examine your story from time to time and see if you might be ready to change it.

fast facts

▶ Inner narrative is the voice you hear in your mind telling you what to believe and replaying these messages on repeat. It doesn't always tell you the truth.

▶ How you remember a traumatic event can be quite different from how someone else remembers the same event.

▶ Get to know *your* version of the traumatic event. How you replay this event in your mind matters. You need to heal from your specific memories.

▶ We can store trauma in our minds as either movie reels or snapshots. Share the images you store with a professional as many times as you need to.

▶ "What if" questions create another part of the story. Feelings of resentment and anger are often part of the "what ifs." It's important to figure out how to release those feelings in order to heal.

Mental Health Professionals

Understanding your client's unique internal narrative is imperative in planning your treatment. To gain a better understanding of the memories they are holding, these are the questions you will want to ask:

- What does your exact version of the traumatic event look like? Share as much detail as possible.
- What is the image you see when you think about your trauma? Is it a movie reel or a snapshot?
- How often do you relive these images?
- When are you most likely to experience them?

Be patient with your client, and encourage them to share their story until they don't feel like they need to share it any longer. By repeatedly sharing details of their event, your client is flooding their trauma and releasing some of its hold over them. With time, the need to share details will lessen. This will be a sign that your client is moving through the grieving process.

Chapter 7

Who's In Charge Here?

When we are no longer able to change a situation,
we are challenged to change ourselves ...

—VIKTOR FRANKL

Remember that image of Jennifer carefully closing her blinds every night before going to bed? This habit became a way of life for her. Without thought, she would complete this task each night. It became routine.

Jennifer feared being assaulted again. This inner narrative of fear played on repeat in her mind, and it rewired her thinking. Jennifer had committed to one idea — she was in real danger. Her mind began to believe that this was an undeniable fact, and her fear narrative created a mental loop that became Jennifer's new truth. But years after the initial attack, was Jennifer really still at risk?

False Alarms

Let's review the facts. As we discussed, trauma impacts brain function. You aren't imagining it. A trauma-impacted brain can lie to us and create new, unhealthy pathways.

After trauma, you may experience fear of being victimized again and/or a hyper-awareness of your surroundings. You're waiting for that other shoe to drop. What do constant hyper-alertness and constant worry do to your mental state? They wear you down physically and emotionally. However, there are ways to avoid this physical drain that we'll discuss throughout this chapter.

WORRY DECEIT

In 2016, researchers from Penn State University conducted a study on constant worry. The study's participants were monitored for thirty days to measure the overall outcome of worrying. All participants had generalized anxiety disorder and were riddled with persistent and uncontrollable worry along with other symptoms (like sleep disturbance and difficulty with concentration), which are familiar to trauma survivors.

In this study, the researchers had participants journal their worries four times per day. The frequency of these journal entries ensured that recent worries were documented while still relatively fresh in the minds of the participants. Participants then reviewed their list of worries each night for thirty days to see if their worries came true. The findings were powerful.

After analyzing the participants' responses, the study found that 91 percent of the documented worries were what the researchers called "false alarms." They were worries that caused panic or concern, yet they never materialized. And for the remaining 9 percent, the worry *did* occur but turned out to have a better-than-expected outcome.[17]

Read those numbers again. Over 90 percent of documented worries are false alarms and never happen. For the other 9 percent, what they worried about did take place, but the outcome was better than expected.

The authors describe this huge difference between worrying and actual outcomes as "worry deceit." Participants experienced strong, concerning thoughts that demanded attention. The threat felt very real. Yet, the study's findings showed that these perceived threats very rarely happen.

ADDRESSING WORRIES

In our daily lives, the perceived threats that we worry about are *almost never real*. This is kind of nice to know and raises a few questions:

- How can this study apply to you and your thoughts?
- Do you ever succumb to "worry deceit"?
- Who is in control — you or your fears?

A brain that has experienced trauma is often susceptible to worry deceit. Maybe the threat is a belief that your boss is going to fire you because you can't show up and work in the same way you did prior to your trauma. Maybe it's the belief that your boyfriend will leave you because you are additionally complicated and needy. Or maybe it's the belief that there is someone lurking outside of your house each night, waiting to retraumatize you or your family.

One exercise I like to use with clients is to have them ask themselves two questions when they are overcome with fear or worry:

1. How likely is it that danger will actually occur while I am running errands today?
2. What would someone I trust have to say about the fear that I'm experiencing right now?

If you can learn to step out of your negative loop and see a situation from a different point of view (even a friend's point of view), you may be able to recognize that what you are experiencing is just worry deceit. Recognizing this fact is the first step in gaining control over these fears.

True or False?

Constant worry also impacts how we think. If worrisome information is repeated again and again, people often start to think of it as the truth. In fact, even when new information is shown to be more accurate, the information that has been heard repeatedly is considered more truthful. Researchers call this the *illusory truth effect.* It's an interesting phenomenon that occurs when the brain is trying to process incoming information.

Here's what happens: When something is easy to process (or familiar), the brain is more likely to think it is true. Consequently, in the real world, our brains view things we can quickly process as more true. So the more we repeat a thought, whether it's positive, negative, or worrisome, the more likely we are to believe it's true. People start to consider how quickly we're able to understand something as a marker of truthfulness.[18]

BELIEFS AND BEHAVIOR

For trauma survivors, the illusory truth effect presents specific challenges. Some thinking or behaviors are motivated by fear resulting from trauma. *Fear can create a negative belief. When a thought is repeated over and over again, our brains believe it to be true, and our behavior may shift, too.*

As embarrassing as it may be, let me share with you a simple example of illusory truth from my own life.

I'm assuming that for most of you, alarm whistles don't sound when you open the garage door to take the car out on errands or to work. Most of you have done this a million times without any negative outcomes. You push the button, and the heavy garage door rolls open.

However, for me, this simple task is more complicated and sprinkled with irrational fears. When I was a teen, my mother told me about a young woman who was injured in a freak accident when opening her garage door. As she stood in the garage waiting for the door to fully open, one of the thick metal springs broke, dislodged from the track, and hit this young woman in the head with such force that it caused long-term neurological damage.

Fear can create a

negative belief.

When a thought

is **repeated** over

and over again,

our brains **believe**

it to be true, and

our **behavior**

may shift, too.

My mother shared the story with me as a reminder to be careful. However, from that day forward, I refused to enter a garage when the door was in motion. I would stand inside the house, open the door just enough so I could snake my arm around the corner, and push the button. I'd yank my arm inside and wait until the groan of the garage door opening had stopped. I would wait a few more seconds, and only then would I feel safe enough to walk into the garage and enter my car. Swiftly, I might add. I figured the quicker I could get under cover, the better.

I behaved this way out of fear that I could be injured. Each and every time I stood on the other side of that door, I reinforced this negative thought. I repeated this behavior so many times that I stopped thinking about the action. I just did it. I was acting on autopilot.

On the rare occasion when I was with a friend (or not at my own home) and was in the garage at the time the garage door was in motion, I felt anxious, almost crossing my fingers and praying that the spring wouldn't break. I had created a new reality where I was in real danger each and every time I was out in the open when a garage door was in motion. All of this was based on one story I was told as a teenager.

This may be a ridiculous example, but it's a real one. And I'm sure that each of us has many ridiculous examples of our own that we could drop into this same formula. Repeating a thought over and over again can make our brains believe it to be true, which can change behavior as well.

Correlations

Have you ever had a lucky sweatshirt that you wear whenever your favorite team is playing? Maybe the team won when you first wore it, and now you're pretty sure that wearing the sweatshirt helps them win. This belief is a good example of an *illusory correlation*. Just because the team won the first time you wore the sweatshirt doesn't mean wearing the sweatshirt resulted in the win. The outcome will be the outcome, regardless of what you wear.

This is true in my example as well. I connected opening the garage door to an impending brain injury. I have yet to find any research that supports this idea. However, do you see how, after repeating that message to myself over and over again, I began to believe it? *The more we are exposed to false information, the more likely we are to believe it.*

Here are some other simple examples:

- You believe that if you wear your lucky hat when gambling, you will be more likely to hit the jackpot.
- Since you were mugged by someone with red hair and your wallet was stolen, you believe that all redheads are shady and cannot be trusted.
- You believe that guns are solely used to harm others; therefore, all gun owners must be bad people.

These are illusory correlations — assumptions that if one thing is true, the other must also be true. However, there is no evidence to back up these claims. Instead, they are repeated thoughts or messages that we receive. The more a message is repeated, the more likely we are to believe it.

Even if beliefs are false, gun violence and trauma survivors can fall into the trap of believing a thought based only on fear. *Your brain believes what you tell it, so be careful what your inner narrative has to say.*

Faulty Wiring

A healthy, uncompromised brain processes thoughts and actions in a linear fashion. It knows that behavior A will lead to behavior B, and by following certain steps, you can attain the desired outcome. Am I confusing you yet? In other words, a healthy brain can easily float from one thought or task to the next with very little effort. This easy flow occurs when we repeat the same pattern over and over again, committing the outcome to memory.

For example, your brain knows that when you open the front door, there will be three steps that you will need to step down before you get to the sidewalk. In time, you walk up and down the stairs so often that your brain has memorized the depth of each step and how to approach them differently when they are wet or icy.

If you repeat this pattern often enough, your brain doesn't have to think about it anymore. Instead, your brain anticipates the steps and is prepared to take action before you have even fully opened the front door and taken your first step outside. In this example, your brain has rewired itself through repetitive thoughts and actions. It has created new neuropathways to accomplish this task quickly and efficiently.

REROUTING

Repetitive thoughts or actions create new neuropathways. Think of these pathways as a kind of road map of the mind. When driving, you follow the most efficient route to get to your destination. The more often you take that route, the easier it becomes. After a while, you may not even have to think about where you're going. You've driven that way so many times you can almost get to your destination on autopilot. You've traveled the route so often that you've created a neuropathway. It's like a rut in the pavement of your brain. Thoughts travel repeatedly from point A (problem) to point B (resolution) with ease on autopilot.

But what happens if fears and false beliefs cause your brain to take detours and make unexpected stops along the route? This rewiring can happen when we overthink or incorporate negative thoughts into our mental processing. It makes the journey longer, harder, and more tiring because you constantly have to stay alert in order to avoid unexpected events.

In this way, a trauma-compromised brain often creates alternate routes. After trauma, we can get caught in unexpected loops, which reroute our mental journey. I explain it to clients as faulty wiring.

Instead of going the quickest way from A to B, you may travel from point A to D to C in order to finally end at B. When this path is repeated over and over, your brain gets used to the longer route. If taken enough times, the result will be a new neuropathway. What once was an easy decision to make now feels like so much effort. Your thoughts have taken many more stops along the way. *Your trauma has rewired your brain.*

TYPICAL REWIRING

This rewiring can happen even in the absence of true trauma. Let's use an everyday example to highlight how new neuropathways can be created. Think about calling a sibling. This action may be as easy as traveling from point A to B on your mind's roadmap. It takes little effort; the ride is pretty short and direct. You can "ride" back and forth without using a map. You know that if you call at the usual time, your sibling is likely to answer, and you can count on them to listen to what you want to share. The end result will be that you feel connected until you are able to call the next time. This action is dependable, and the task isn't frightening.

However, if you add a negative thought to the task of calling your sibling, your route becomes less direct, and your mental ride to point B becomes much more complicated. There are roadblocks and detours. Maybe your sibling hasn't been as comforting on past calls as you'd hoped. You have begun to create a story, making assumptions like she is being selfish or doesn't love you. Maybe you spend a lot of time pondering this negative thought. This repeated thought process has now created a new, tangled neuropathway that adds these negative detours. Instead of the direct A to B, your brain now goes from point A to D to C and back to B. This route is not as comfortable, and you are much more depleted by the time you get to the destination — actually making the call.

If your brain follows this route often enough, you will create a new neuropathway. You will change your thinking. Eventually, it's not the act of calling your sibling that is challenging, but just the thought of it that elicits a negative response (this could include heart racing, sweating, or feelings of sadness).

REWIRING AFTER TRAUMA

That's an everyday example. For a trauma survivor, this rerouting can happen more easily and create even more distress. For years after the attack, Jennifer fought vigilantly to adjust to her new lifestyle. As we have discussed, Jennifer's losses were many. She was paralyzed and no longer able to move freely. She also lost her home, custody of her child, her independence, and her security. Now, Jennifer recalls one period in time when the emotional and physical pain had just become too great. She was fatigued. The daily struggle just to maintain her existence had pushed her into hopelessness. "What could life possibly have to offer me, and what do I have to contribute?" she would wonder.

Jennifer told herself, "I should just let go." Her thoughts began to circle around what it would feel like to "let go," the peace she would experience, the pain that she wouldn't have to face daily. In her fatigue, Jennifer's repetitive thoughts created a new neuropathway. Her brain rewired itself. She believed that dying was the best option — both for herself and those around her.

Four years after the shooting, Jennifer attempted to take her life when she grabbed prescription medications and vodka and laid down to take a nap. At that time, Jennifer's illusory truth led her to believe that there was nothing in life that was worth living if it meant living with the pain she was experiencing. She believed that she would never regain her lost sense of self.

She was worried that she would be a burden to others forever. She didn't want to be something else that others needed to take care of. Her worry deceit was in control. She was experiencing recurring physical pain that she believed would never cease. Jennifer's mind had rewired itself.

Thank goodness Jennifer survived. Today, Jennifer's life is full. She's worked hard both physically and emotionally to become the incredible woman that she is now. She has exceeded her own expectations, and she has dedicated her life to helping others achieve incredible milestones. Jennifer is powerful, to say the least. But, back then, her negative messages were playing on repeat.

CONTROL THE NARRATIVE

It is important to remember that just because you think something doesn't mean it is true. Also, just because a frightening event has happened doesn't mean it will happen again. As we learned in the study above, 91 percent of the things we worry about never happen.

Remember, both positive and negative thoughts create a mental roadmap (a.k.a. neuropathway). The more energy you put into a thought and the more you repeat it, the deeper the pathway will be embedded in your mind.

How are you using your inner narrative? Be careful. Your brain believes what you tell it. Choose your messaging wisely.

fast facts

▸ Trauma impacts the brain. You are not imagining it.

▸ When thoughts are repeated over and over again, your brain believes they are true.

▸ Constant worry and repetitive thoughts impact how your brain functions. Repetitive thoughts, whether positive or negative, create new thought patterns called neuropathways.

▸ Worry deceit is the discrepancy between what you are worrying about and what actually happens. A recent study shows that 91 percent of what we worry about only very rarely comes true.

▸ Faulty wiring occurs when a trauma-compromised brain gets caught up in an unhealthy mental loop. This creates a new neuropathway and rewires your brain.

Mental Health Professionals

These concepts are complicated, even for some of us. Remember that your clients are expending a great amount of energy just in grieving and processing their daily lives. Brain fog is common. Attempt to explain brain functioning to them in small doses and only when you feel they are ready. Explain and discuss complex terms in a way that is easily relatable. I use an analogy of a roadmap when describing neuropathways and faulty wiring. Try to find an analogy that will speak to your specific client's mindset.

Understanding post-trauma brain function is not an essential part of healing for all of your clients. However, it can be empowering. Psychoeducation on neuropathways and brain functioning is particularly helpful if a client begins to exhibit shame or frustration about their thoughts.

Some clients may even become obsessive about their fears or beliefs. If this occurs, begin by trying to help them understand how brain rewiring can occur after a trauma. Remind them that, in some ways, they are driving this rewiring, *but it is a process that can be reversed with intentional messaging.* Cognitive behavioral therapy (CBT) is a helpful technique to use when working to regain power over our thoughts.

Chapter 8

Triggers

Life is made up of three things:
uncertainty, pain, and a ton of work.

—PHIL STUTZ

The word *trigger* is interesting — particularly given the topic of this book. It can have two meanings. The first, of course, is the lever that is pulled to set off a firearm, often inflicting harm. The second is something that sets off an emotional response related to past trauma.

A trauma trigger can be anything that reminds you of your traumatic event. It can be people, places, smells, sounds, or even music that takes your mind right back to a moment in that event. These triggers are often involuntary, and so is your body's response to them.

As both a gun violence survivor and mental health professional, I don't particularly like either version of the word trigger. It's no secret that the trigger of a weapon can create serious, life-altering damage. However, many people are unaware of the ways a trauma trigger can also cause pain, fear, and worry. In this chapter, we'll talk about this definition of trigger. Understanding trauma triggers is an important part of the healing journey.

Triggered

The physical response to a trigger can show up in many ways. It might be an upset stomach or trouble eating. It could be disturbed sleep or the constant feeling of fatigue or exhaustion. Maybe it's a pounding heart, rapid breathing, or feeling shaky. Remember the four F's — fight, flight, flee, or fawn? Your body's response to a trigger can easily take you back to that state of heightened awareness.

I suspect most of you can easily identify what triggers you, taking you back to that state of fight or flight. For me, it was anything that had to do with a gun. I could be driving on the highway and see a billboard advertising an upcoming gun show, and I would feel my grip tighten on the steering wheel and my jaw clench. I live in the Wild West, so seeing those billboards isn't unusual. I admit that I almost always spewed some pretty gnarly curse words whenever I saw one. The same thing would happen if I passed a shooting range. A hunting magazine? Same response. The list of potential triggers goes on and on, and the list of creative cursing was longer.

More times than I can count, I would find myself in a movie theater, and without being fully prepared for it, an epic shoot-out would erupt on the giant screen. You know the kinds of scenes I'm talking about — several high-powered weapons, bullets flying in every direction, and a battle that seems to go on forever and ever. I would turn my head to the side to stare at the theater wall or look down at my chest. If I felt like I could own my discomfort in front of everyone, I would physically cover my eyes.

At the time, I don't think I realized that I was holding my breath during these scenes, but I most certainly was. Once I heard the firing stop, I would slowly raise my eyes or drop the hand shielding my view. My shoulders would drop, too, and I could finally exhale. By the end of the scene, I was totally detached from the movie, no longer entertained. The one place I loved to go and get away from the stressors of my world had been stolen from me.

I was so affected by just the idea of guns that when I had my first child, I vowed to *never* allow him to play with any toy that even resembled a gun! There were no cowboy suits with holsters or wooden rifles that shot rubber bands. No police costumes. You name it.

My family was advised that I wouldn't allow my son to even pretend to have a gun. I mean, I made a big deal about it. I remember my mom smirking at me, like, "Okay, Jill, we'll see how that goes. You're being over-protective." This was just another reminder to me that she didn't appreciate how much our kidnapping had burrowed into the fabric of who I was.

But damn it! My mom was right. No matter how hard I tried and how much I tried to protect him by not allowing toy weapons, that little boy just found his own way of pretending. I swear, if you gave him a blade of grass, he would figure out how to point it at a target and go, "Pew,

pew!" I have no deep psychological hypothesis for this. I'm not going to present you with data or research as to why this happened. I just know it exists. I chalked it up to "boys will be boys."

I remember one specific evening when my husband and I were cleaning the kitchen after dinner. Our son must have been eight years old at the time. I was bending over to place a dish into the dishwasher, and when I stood up, I saw him point his finger in the direction of my head and pull the imaginary trigger.

Now, I know he was playing. He was smiling and zipping around the room. There was no harmful intention or even awareness of what he had done. But I stood there, frozen. I stopped breathing. I instantly wanted to curl up in a ball and cry. I was taken back to that moment of having a gun held to my head when I was a child. The emotion was just so strong and involuntary. Fortunately, the urge not to scare my son was even greater, so I did not curl up or cry. Instead, moments later, I quietly left the room and broke down. I was physically reacting to a trigger.

My husband followed me, knowing I was upset. I remember him alluding to the fact that I may need to get some real help, like from a professional, instead of relying on myself to "handle it." It was obvious that whatever I was doing to heal myself wasn't enough.

When it came to "protecting" my son from guns, I was fighting an impossible fight. Instead, what I was doing was only increasing his desire for something he was told he couldn't have. So, I learned to adapt. As he got older, he was allowed to play with Nerf Super Soakers or Junior Nerf Blasters — you know, the kind with the foam bullets.

I just had a conversation with him first to be sure he was aware of my stance on guns and that these were toys.

There were certain lines I wouldn't cross. No laser guns. No Nerf guns with rapid fire. I was bargaining with myself, making myself feel like I was still taking some sort of stance. It all sounds so stupid now. But at the time, I was doing the best I could. The biggest lesson from this parenting journey was that I needed to get control of the trauma instead of allowing the trauma to control me!

What's Your Trigger?

A trigger is specific to you and your individual story. In my example, it's fairly obvious why the image and sound of guns triggered me. Your trigger will be related to the trauma you experienced, but it might be more subliminal than mine. For instance, it could be the smell of curry because, on the night that you received the news of your brother's sudden death, you had dined out at an Indian restaurant with some coworkers. That might sound unlikely to you, but the trigger-to-trauma relationship can actually be that random. And regardless of whether it is obvious or unexpected, it can still pack a heavy punch.

This reminds me of a story that my mentor Frank shared with me. He had worked with a client who lost her son to suicide. Sometime after the loss, this client had a full-blown panic episode one afternoon while visiting with a dear friend of hers. She called him, upset and confused. She didn't understand what had caused her such sudden anguish, and she was afraid it could happen

A **trigger**

is **specific**

to you

and your

individual

story.

again at any time. The fear of a recurring panic attack was keeping her from leaving her home.

Frank asked his client to slow down, back up, and recount everything that she could about that visit with her friend. She began with high-level details. It was a pleasant summer afternoon. She and her friend sat in the living room and enjoyed some tea. She reported that they were just catching up when she was stricken with this sudden grief. Physically shaken, she dropped her tea, shattering the glass it was served in. She was still confused, not understanding the sudden onset of such strong emotions. She felt out of control.

Again, Frank asked her to slow down and think back. He wanted even more detail about what she had experienced that afternoon. He asked her to think about her surroundings. What were the colors in the room and the scents in the house? With his coaching, she was able to recall something she had forgotten about altogether. She said that shortly before her panic episode, she had heard the faint whistle of a train passing nearby.

Frank was able to identify the sound of the train as the trigger. He knew that on the night of her son's death, she had gotten a call from the hospital saying that there had been a horrible accident and she needed to come immediately. Unfortunately, the hospital was an hour away. Driving in sheer terror and desperate to make it to her son's side, she had recounted feeling as if it was the slowest car ride of her life. And then she got stuck at a train crossing. With each boxcar that went by, she became more and more inconsolable.

Hearing a train in the distance as she visited with her friend on that summer afternoon had taken her right back to that night. She may not have made any conscious connection, but her body was responding to the sound of the train and the memory of the night her son died.

Your trigger may not be obvious. There may not be a neon sign pointing at what it is that sends you over the edge. You may have several triggers. This is also very normal. *What's important is that you take time to identify what triggers you.* You will benefit the most from what we discuss in the sections that follow if you take the time to identify your personal triggers before moving on to the next chapter of this book.

FACE YOUR FEAR

Generally, we avoid the things that frighten us. I often use the example of an old horror film. You know, the ones where the bogeyman was always lurking outside? He is hiding behind the bushes or peeking in the window as the woman is sitting on her sofa watching a movie. Inevitably, the bogeyman is discovered, and the woman scrambles to find a hiding place in the house. (Why do they always hide under a bed or in a closet?)

The story always ends the same way — the bogeyman somehow makes his way into the house and discovers the hiding place. I've always wondered what would happen if, instead of hiding, the woman just opened the door and asked the bogeyman to come in for a chat. If the end result is going to be the same, why not first ask him to come in for a conversation? Why not try to take some control of the situation?

Now, let's take your fear and make it the bogeyman. You can run, hide, and try to avoid it for as long as you want. Yet, more than likely, the effects of this running will eventually catch up with you. The end result will be the same — you will still experience massive discomfort, but you will only have prolonged the duration. I want you to open the door to the bogeyman (your fears) and ask him to come in for a chat. Maybe you can change the ending. Facing these fears gets you closer to healing.

The Next Mass Shooting

It's inevitable. We will all turn on the television or scan the notifications on our phones in the upcoming days or weeks and learn about the latest mass shooting. The story will often unfold in real time in front of us. We'll learn about the victims, the weapons used, and how the emergency response could have been handled differently. The formula hasn't changed much since the media first started reporting on mass shootings.

These events used to set me back for days! They were another trigger —known to commonly impact gun violence survivors. Sometimes, I hadn't even heard about the latest shooting before I started receiving texts from concerned friends: "Thinking of you." "Love you." "Just checking in. You okay?"

This would signal to me that something bad had happened. Before I could find a television, I would begin to feel the physical symptoms of being triggered. I'd be anxious. I'd easily lose focus on whatever I was doing before. And I'd begin to feel deep anger. (That intense cursing would surface again.) The show of concern from my friends was a sign that they recognized the hold these events would have on me.

This way of living became the new normal. A new shooting event triggered a new response. I'd slowly recover, and just when I'd begin to trust the world again, another shooting would occur. After years of this cycle, my trauma response morphed into more anger than fear. It was a loop that needed to be broken. Perhaps you've found yourself in a similar cycle.

You may have noticed that I used the past tense when describing my triggers. That's intentional. Triggers are something of the *past* for me. I rarely experience them these days. I've done the work to gain control over them. The best way for you to begin doing the same is to identify your personal triggers and understand them. Until you are able to specifically identify your triggers, you can't begin the work to regain control and take away the power that these triggers have over you.

Triggers Are Everywhere

Because of the prevalence of gun violence and the extensive media coverage it receives, even individuals who have not personally been victimized can experience the effects of triggers. For example, in October 2023, a headline caught my eye. An article detailed how dozens of people were hurt while attending a peace rally at the University of Florida. The story recounted that a young

WHEN YOU ARE THE BREAKING NEWS

Gun violence has become an alarmingly more common event in our society and lives. Whether it's another mass shooting or a sudden death, the media is quick to report the incident in great detail. This coverage deeply impacts immediate survivors. Maybe your trauma was reported in the media. What was once a private family matter is now being seen on a screen by hundreds, if not thousands, of strangers.

If this has been your experience, know that media coverage of your traumatic event can complicate your healing process. In my experience, the more a trauma is in the media, the more likely it is that the survivor's grief process is delayed. When a family's trauma plays out in the media (television, social media, etc.), others feel like they have a say in how it was handled or what could have happened differently. On top of everything else, the victims can feel watched and judged.

This ongoing coverage and feedback often stalls any real processing of the trauma. When too many people have too many opinions about what you should do next, it becomes a distraction and can complicate the brain's reasoning. A trauma survivor is merely working to put one foot in front of the other. When too much information is thrown at a trauma survivor from too many sources, it causes additional distress. No one can effectively grieve when confronting their story repeatedly. Know that this is an added challenge in your healing process.

woman at the rally had passed out while in the crowd. The crowd was large and noisy. When rally participants heard loud noises and saw this young lady fall, chaos ensued. One rally participant became spooked, assuming that the young woman had been shot. This panic spread, and soon, hundreds of young adults were running for shelter, fearing there was a shooter nearby.

In their desperate run to safety, dozens of participants were trampled, resulting in broken bones and other injuries. It was later discovered that the crowd was never in danger. There was no shooter or threat. Instead, an unexpected loud noise, coupled with the motion of a young woman fainting, created a sudden alarm. People assumed they were at risk of being victims of gun violence, and an entire crowd was triggered into a flight response. This is an example of the anticipatory fear that many of us now experience. It's a new reality that our culture lives with as a result of the seemingly endless stream of gun violence events.

For some, it doesn't take loud sounds and sudden action to create a trigger. Student anxiety is at an all-time high, and experts believe that social media is at least partially responsible. The constant bombardment of news stories and images has left many children and teens feeling generally unsafe.

This feeling of being unsafe can be compounded by lockdown drills. Since the Columbine High School mass shooting, these drills have become common, with many states requiring at least two per year. Some experts believe that lockdown exercises can do as much harm as good. They are a constant reminder of what could happen, which can be a trigger for students and make them feel even more fearful and anxious.[19]

Triggers create pain and anxiety. There is no way around this discomfort — the only way out is through it. So buckle up and get started on the work that is necessary to get you to the other side.

▸ Triggers are both emotional and physical. They are often involuntary.

▸ Triggers make us feel as if we are no longer in control.

▸ Avoiding a fear/trigger will only prolong its impact on your life.

▸ We heal by finding small ways to regain control of our world.

▸ Working to explore and understand our specific triggers will help remove their power over us.

Mental Health Professionals

Triggers are unique to each client. Be cautious not to assume that a client must be fearful of one thing rather than another. Their individual story and how it is stored in their memory will dictate which images, smells, sounds, etc., are particularly troubling for them. I used the example of one of my own triggers — guns. That's an obvious trigger, given my story. I implore you to be more creative and explorative when helping your clients identify their triggers. Think of the example my mentor Frank shared with me about his client and trains. This client was unaware and even mystified to discover that so much physical distress could result from the faint sound of a train.

Your primary focus during this phase of treatment is to help your client unearth the core of their fear. Where is this trigger coming from? Identifying this trigger is empowering for your client. We can't heal what we can't see!

Subsequently, help your client understand that by learning how to manage these triggers, they will begin to regain a sense of control. So much of healing from trauma is about the fight for regaining control and power over our own thoughts and, therefore, our lives. Assure them that there is hope. This step of identifying triggers gets us one step closer to providing them with the techniques they need to overcome their specific situation.

Chapter 9

Talk About It

A pain shared is a pain halved.

—KEVIN HINES

I've often heard clients say, "No one wants to hear my story anymore. I am a broken record." When I hear this statement, I see it as a sign of a survivor approaching isolation, and isolation leads to depression. They feel like others are impatient and tired of listening to them retell their story one more time. They feel like maybe they should be "over it" — but they're not.

You may feel the same. You feel that others can't relate, which makes it hard to talk about what happened. And, after a certain number of weeks or months, it seems like life has moved on for everyone except you. You feel as if you are on an island all alone, so you stop sharing. You put on a mask and attempt to continue living — *attempt* being the keyword.

You wake up each day, mask up, and engage in daily life. You converse about things that are of no interest to you. Eventually, you feel like you are living a lie. Internally, you are repressing memories, sadness, confusion, and anxieties that you have had to choose not to share with others.

Instead of healing from your experience, you are allowing those hidden-away emotions to fester and take over. Like an infection, if these are not cleaned out, you can eventually become sick. I mean this both figuratively and literally, as we will see with some of the healing journeys described within these pages. For these reasons and more, it's important to get comfortable talking about your trauma.

I describe it to clients in a slightly more descriptive way. I ask them to think of unexpressed stress and anxiety as pieces of trash that fill our mental trash can. What happens when you fill that can, push the trash down, and keep piling more trash on top of it? It eventually spills over. Take out your trash.

Repeat, Repeat, Repeat

When I say share your trauma and tell your story, I mean tell your story again and again. At first, it may not feel comfortable to keep repeating what happened but do it anyway. *Repeat your story to anyone who will listen.*

This type of repetition is a technique that is part of a larger method called "flooding." Each time you share your experience and mentally visit that frightening space, you slowly dilute its power over you. If you seek the assistance of a therapist and spend each session telling the same story for months, you are not wasting anyone's time. You are flooding in an environment that feels safe to you. Hopefully, in time, the version of your story will change some. Maybe even become less powerful. That is effective.

Sharing your story cleanses the trauma from the front of your memory. You dilute the power it has over your thoughts. If keeping something a secret gives it power, then the opposite is also true. Bringing an emotion or memory out into the light releases its hold on you.

Flooding is the process of exposing yourself to your greatest fear for a prolonged period of time until your brain and body eventually calm down.

HOW YOU TELL IT

Maybe you're ready to give this a try. How do you begin? When processing your trauma and attempting to flood, what matters most is that you share your emotions and experiences in a way that is healthy and easy for you. For some, sharing out loud has never been easy or comfortable. Why would it be any easier after a traumatic event?

A mentor of mine suggests that you express yourself in one of three ways and then repeat it:

- Speak it
- Draw it
- Write it
- Repeat it — again and again

Bringing an

emotion or

memory out

into the *light*

releases its

hold on you.

All of these modalities work. Pick the one that is most comfortable for you, and get in the habit of practicing it weekly. Journal several days a week before you go to bed. Sit at the kitchen table and scribble, draw, or express on paper what you're feeling. Tell a friend or family member. Just make time to release your story and emotions as often as you can!

WHO YOU TELL

This is an opportunity to expand your circle and expand your expectations. You don't have to confide in your family. Sometimes, they are too close to the event, and they could be processing their own traumatic response. You don't have to confide in another trauma survivor. Just because they may be able to relate to what you went through doesn't mean they can be a good listener. Often, interactions with people you least expect can leave you feeling the most consoled.

Don't hide your new anxieties or fears from others just to protect them. After all, being honest about new insecurities may be well received. And if it is not, at least you have started the practice of sharing. Owning your discomfort is part of the healing process.

For instance, say your trauma story involved a vehicle, and you've now developed a fear of driving downtown or being the passenger in a car doing the same. You've been asked to join some friends on an excursion downtown for the afternoon. What should you do?

You have a few choices:

- You could say nothing about your fears, decline that trip, and stay safely at home, yet miss out on an experience — isolating yourself.

- You could say nothing, agree to take the trip downtown, and be riddled with anxiety, sweating, and gripping at the dashboard, having expended a lot of energy before even making it to your destination.
- Or you could tell your fellow passengers that since your traumatic event, you have developed a real fear of driving downtown. You could explain that you would like to go with them, but they can expect you to be a little anxious when driving to and from your destination.

What if you choose the last option? You may not expect talking about it and actually getting into a car to head downtown will help you feel better. However, not only does this allow you to speak your truth (cleansing some of your trauma), but it also re-engages you with the world, combatting isolation. It turns out the last option is a step in the right direction and can get you closer to healing.

If you need to share your story with others repeatedly, don't be afraid. They'll understand, and if they don't, find other people. It may be beneficial to share small doses of your traumatic memories with several different groups. Holding someone else's trauma can be overwhelming for some. That's understandable. Either way, keep telling your story. *It's a necessary step in your healing journey.*

LAURA – A CAUTIONARY TALE

At the beginning of the book, I introduced you to Laura, a young law student who had lost her mother to suicide. I shared that it took several years for Laura to seek real psychological help for herself. She spent the first few years putting the needs of her surviving family ahead of her own. She was on damage control. In addition, Laura was also masterful at staying focused on her rigorous studies. Studying was a great escape from her very painful reality. Maybe it was a flight response to her trauma? Rather than flooding and sharing her emotions with others, she kept them tightly controlled, which left her anxious, irritable, and exhausted.

Laura graduated college and started law school in a new city only months after her mother's death. She was able to create a new identity for herself, getting to know the other students in her program without mentioning her mother's suicide. In this fresh environment, very few people knew about her mother's sudden death, so she could avoid talking about it. "I don't open up to anyone," she told me during her first year of law school. "I don't have time to get upset or break down." She tried to hide her truth. In some ways, Laura hoped that by *not* talking about her trauma, she could control its impact.

But she was also afraid of the pain that would be associated with even whispering details of the events of her mother's suicide. She was still incapable of sharing her horrors with others or finding a way to heal. Laura knew she needed to share her story. She worked with me for a short time, but life got busy. She knew she should be honest with her friends and talk to her mentor, but she was unable to speak the words. Laura wasn't ready or able to work on her healing at that time.

IGNORING YOUR PAIN

Several years after graduating from law school, Laura was diagnosed with lymphoma. She was in her late twenties and had worked tirelessly to obtain her degree and overcome every obstacle set in front of her.

I've always wondered if things would have been different for Laura if she had been able to process and emote instead of function in a constant state of damage control. Laura was good at hiding her painful emotions behind a mask and still getting everything done. However, when the mask becomes a permanent part of the wardrobe, we put ourselves at greater risk of causing detrimental effects on the body. Laura is not alone. So many trauma survivors respond in a similar way.

As you recall, we talked about how the body physically responds to trauma earlier in the book. In fact, decades of research have found that when the stress response remains activated for long periods of time, it can lead to imbalances in the body.[20] Ultimately, these imbalances related to chronic stress have been associated with serious health issues, including heart attack and stroke, weakened immune system, susceptibility to cancer, chronic headache, sleep disturbance, anxiety, depression, and more.

In retrospect, I wish Laura had been able to get support for herself sooner to relieve some of the trauma-related stress she kept so close to her chest.

Help Others Help You

Try to remind yourself that, for the most part, others want to help you. They often just don't know how. If you go inward, stop sharing, or get used to putting on that mask with them, they may have no other choice but to move on and assume that you are doing okay or that you no longer want their help.

I'm about to ask you to do something hard: Be a role model for caregivers and friends by telling them what you need.

I know you're tired!

I understand that you hardly have the energy to complete the bare minimum at times.

I get that the thought of being a role model for anyone probably makes you want to reach out and slap me. I get it.

However, if you stop communicating your needs and hold back emotions, it's dangerous — both for you and your relationships. Sometimes, caregivers just don't know what they haven't been told.

A caveat. There will be some people who just don't know how to respond to your trauma. That's just how the cookie crumbles. That doesn't make them bad people. What I have learned in my years of working with survivors is that people who don't know how to respond usually weren't taught by a caregiver or parental figure.

Move on from them if you can. Don't spend too much time obsessing over their reaction or lack of reaction to you. Don't take it personally. They just don't know any better. If you choose, you can circle back at a later date to address your disappointments. For now, find the people you can share with and rely on.

You are not a burden. Don't let anyone make you feel like you are.

Sharing your experience and engaging with others can help. It's important to share your emotions and experiences in a way that is healthy and easy for you, whether that's through writing, speaking, or drawing.

fast facts

▸ Talking about your trauma is important. It helps cleanse the traumatic memories and dilute their power over you. Do not attempt to hold on to your traumatic memories to spare others.

▸ Flooding is the process of exposing yourself to your greatest fear for a prolonged period of time until your brain and body eventually calm down. It is a helpful way of gaining control over your trauma.

▸ Chronic stress can lead to a state of imbalance in the body and has been associated with a number of negative effects on health.

▸ You may have to ask your support system for what you need. You may have to tell them very specifically what is most helpful and what is not helpful. That's okay. Odds are that they will appreciate the guidance.

Mental Health Professionals

It's not uncommon for trauma survivors to want to spend months retelling their story or evaluating their experience. Don't be surprised if many of your sessions in the first few months feel like a repeat of the session before. This is okay.

You do not need to force your client to move forward. Let them share their story until they feel they no longer need to tell it. If a client has healthy coping skills, this retelling may not take long. If possible, allow them to lead this portion of the process. Remember, there may be no one else they feel they can genuinely express the details of their trauma with.

Help your client be creative when it comes to expressing the pain from their experience. For some, talk therapy is challenging. Think outside of the box. Does your client emote more easily through art? Ask them to create a musical playlist for you that best describes how they are feeling. What about nature sessions? If it's more comfortable for your client and available to you, take a walk around the neighborhood near your office while you are talking about a particularly difficult experience. In this day and age, you do not need a sofa and a chair to perform therapy. Meet your client where they are with the goal of helping them to expel their trauma.

Chapter 10

Your Identity

I assure you, I'm not put together at all.
Nor am I broken.
I'm recovering — finding the beautiful in
the ugly and stitching it into my life.

—RACHEL WOLCHIN

A life is a collection of experiences, both good and bad. In my own healing, I've found the analogy of a quilt to be really helpful. The day of my kidnapping was only one patch in the entire quilt of my life's events. Sure, the kidnapping was an important event, and in many ways, it molded me. However, I also have so many other life-changing events to memorialize. Most of them are great and filled with incredible joy! They each represent a patch as well. All of these patches, when put together, make the complete quilt that is my life. One patch does not create a quilt.

Sometimes, we think we are working toward healing, but in reality, we aren't making much headway. Often, this is because we aren't doing it effectively. Healing is certainly not a one-size-fits-all endeavor. There is no magic formula or checklist. Healing is unique to each individual's experience. We've just talked about the importance of sharing and repeating your story. You also have to develop personal coping strategies by figuring out what is or is not working. Then, you're ready to develop a plan to heal effectively.

This is the chapter where I get real with you. It's just me (the trauma survivor and mental health professional) talking to you (the trauma survivor). In addition to owning your individual story, in order to continue to move forward, you need to examine what you are telling yourself about who you are now.

How You Identify Yourself

Responses we get from others can change how we see ourselves. And as we all now know, the brain believes what you tell it. This is why working on how you identify yourself is so important. After trauma, you may feel like you're living two lives simultaneously, the "before trauma" you and the "after trauma" you. This can leave you with a lot of questions. What does this new identity look like? How do I define myself post-trauma? Do I present myself differently to the world?

After the shooting that caused Jennifer to be paralyzed, she recounted that people looked at her differently. "They were hesitant to approach me," she said. She began to believe that she was responsible for making people feel uncomfortable. She said others' reactions created a belief in her that she was "too much for people to handle." She began to retreat, becoming shy. She was building a false sense of self that was based on outside responses. She was no longer the same Jennifer.

When talking about losing her self-image and how this self-image "defined everything" in her life, Jennifer explained, "I lived with an overwhelming feeling that I was broken."

Who Are You Now?

How do you think of yourself now that you've lived through this life-changing event? Think about these questions:

- *Do you consider yourself to be broken?* Have you referred to yourself as broken in the same way that Jennifer did for the first few years after her event? If you believe you are broken, do you believe you are incapable of mending?
- *Do you believe that you are a weaker version of yourself post-trauma?* What your body has attempted to process is gigantic. It can leave you feeling depleted and as though you are functioning on an empty tank at times. Do you confuse this fatigue for weakness?
- *Have you created a competition around your pain and trauma?* Has what you have experienced and overcome become a type of badge of honor that you wear? The *"my situation is worse than yours"* mentality is sometimes used to try to gain some sense of control or status back into your life.

Finally, ask yourself, *do I define myself as a victim?* Be honest with yourself here because it really matters. I want you to take some time for self-examination. Really review your feelings about how you define yourself now that you have been personally impacted by a traumatic situation. Maybe get out a piece of paper and jot down five to ten phrases that you use to identify yourself now, post-trauma. Don't put too much thought into it; instead, let the answers flow freely and honestly.

None of these are labels you have asked for. You didn't want to be a part of this event, which changed how you look at the world and how others may look at you. However, how you identify yourself can add to the trauma's effect, and this time, you are the one responsible.

Learn to Rewire

Remember that chapter on faulty wiring? No worries if you don't. Here's a short recap — *with repetitive thinking, we can rewire our brains.*

Jennifer's story provides an example of this. After the shooting, she repeatedly received responses from others that she perceived to mean she was broken and frightening to be around. In time, she began to think that maybe she was too much for people to handle. Maybe she was, indeed, "too broken."

Jennifer entertained this thought long enough that she began to believe that it was true. She had rewired her brain to believe that she was broken, weak, and too much for others to handle. This became one more thing she needed to heal.

DEFINE YOURSELF

How you define yourself matters. After trauma, it's natural to feel you've lost some control over your life and surroundings. You were, after all, the victim of a horrific experience. But how do you move past this feeling? I've found that clients who identify as victims continue to feel a loss of control in their lives. They feel like they can't change the story, and it seems as if bad things keep happening to them no matter what they do.

In time, believing you are a victim can turn into a dangerous mental slippery slope. Individuals who have a victim mentality quickly believe that the world is out to get them. They have thoughts of, "What did I do to deserve this?" This theme becomes a loop that plays on repeat in their minds, and the end result can be resentment — toward others and toward life.

Often, this negative viewpoint or victim mindset after trauma is a result of flawed coping strategies. This can lead you to believe that things *just happen* to you and you have no responsibility for what happens in your life. You can come to feel that you were never in control from the beginning, so why would you think you can control anything going forward? Why even try?

Others may offer suggestions to help, but you can find a list of reasons why those things wouldn't work. This can leave those who are offering help feeling frustrated or confused. If this sounds like you, you may also feel frustrated and confused, questioning why you continue to behave in this way.

The simple truth is that there are probably some secondary benefits that make it hard to change from a victim's mindset. You might gain sympathy or attention as a result of your distress. Maybe you feel relieved that others are offering help or validation. You may feel that your victim identity is what makes you stand out from others. You also might not be comfortable with the idea of feeling vulnerable again, so it's easier not to take risks. You know that doing the work to overcome your trauma will entail some difficult thoughts and conversations — work that will likely require you to be vulnerable. That, my friends, can be scary.

So, let's reframe how you view yourself. Imagine the volume of my voice rising as you read these words. They are that important.

You are not a victim for life! You were a victim ONCE.
(Repeat that as often as necessary.)

Can you feel the difference that's possible with those words? See how it can change your mindset? Reframing your thoughts in this way frees you up for the possibility of hope and joy. Even if you feel that you have been victimized more times than you care to count, I would argue that the above statement still applies. You do not have to be a victim for life. You can choose a different path forward.

No one ever said your trauma needs to be a life sentence.

Let Go of Victimhood

Here's our reality — we've lost a lot as a result of this experience.

We've lost our sense of safety and the effortless ability to trust others without thinking they may have ulterior motives.

We've lost the idea of a carefree future self. We aren't sure we can ever go to a public place or revisit a place that triggers us again without being anxious or feeling the need to flee.

We've lost the sense of safety for our kids and family. Some of us may spill our anxieties onto our partners or children, making them feel unnecessarily anxious about their own worlds.

And for those physically or cognitively injured during trauma, physical freedoms have been lost. The future is no longer the way it was once envisioned.

What I say next may surprise you. Yes, you have changed, but it doesn't have to be for the worse.

More than a Survivor

Being a trauma survivor is not an all-or-nothing title. Your driver's license will not read Jane Doe, Gun Violence Survivor. You are multifaceted. This event feels big. It *is* big. However, it does not define you, and you do not need to solely identify as your trauma. Yes. You are a gun violence survivor. But you are so much more than that.

Before the event, you were someone with purpose and desires. You had hobbies you were interested in, goals you were working toward, and skills you were known for. You were someone's brother, boyfriend, mother, auntie, or best friend. You can still be all of those things — and also be a survivor of gun violence. Although this event has reshaped you, it really is just an addition to the events that have already occurred in your life and the ones that are yet to come in your future. Remember, your trauma is only one patch in your quilt.

Give yourself permission to be unique, individual, and multi-layered. You can be a gun violence survivor AND a skilled athlete, loving sibling, helpful caretaker, successful salesperson, advocate for others, passionate musician, goal-oriented student — you name it.

You can be all of it. You *are* all of it. Don't shorten your credentials to only include the word "survivor." You are SO much more.

fast facts

- ▶ You get to choose your identity. No one gets to decide for you.

- ▶ How you see yourself matters. It can shape the trajectory of your healing. You are more than your trauma.

- ▶ Trauma can leave you feeling broken and weak. It may seem that you have lost your true sense of self. Give yourself credit for your strengths as well.

- ▶ Take control of your narrative. You can be a trauma survivor and also be so much more.

- ▶ Your trauma is only one patch in your quilt of life.

- ▶ Pay attention to what you have gained through your trauma. I promise those things exist.

Mental Health Professionals

Words matter in your work with a trauma survivor. In particular, the words they choose to identify themselves with will impact their healing. Pay attention to how your client refers to themselves. And in time, help them to see how they are so much more.

Help your client understand that many emotions and experiences can co-exist. They can feel deep sadness about the loss of one child while simultaneously deeply loving and supporting another child. They can be a mom grieving a lost child *and* a loving mom to their surviving children. They can experience real fulfillment in their workday and still feel empty when they come home to an empty house. They can be a passionate employee and struggle with the effects of trauma at the same time. They are multifaceted. Labeling themselves as exclusively one thing or another (griever, victim, broken) can create a new neuropathway. This will be another hurdle for them to overcome. Our goal is to remove any additional hurdles that we can.

A caveat here: I am not opposed to the term "victim." Be careful not to send the message that you dislike it. You may create a disconnect between yourself and your client. Your client *has* been victimized. They have now been given that title by their peers and neighbors. There is validity to it. Our job is to educate them so they can see that *they are more* than just that and to help teach them skills to avoid living into that definition.

Tools *for* Healing

Chapter 11

The Gift of Perspective

*If you don't think that you have anything to be grateful for,
keep looking. Because you don't just receive optimism.
You can't wait for things to be great and then be grateful
for that. You've got to behave in a way that promotes that.*

—MICHAEL J. FOX

Perspective has been a recurring theme in my office. I have specialized in suicide loss for over twenty years. I have listened to hundreds of individuals grappling to make sense of the way their loved one died. Some survivors say that suicide is the most unspeakable loss. I will say that it can be one of the most complicated, for sure. Yet amidst the gut-wrenching pain, bewildering confusion, and deep longing, many discover the gift of perspective.

Depending on where you are in your healing, you may have some questions. How could your trauma result in anything positive? However, what I am told over and over again by survivors is it can. They just don't care about the little, insignificant things in life anymore. They recognize that these things don't really matter. They aren't caught up in gossip or concerned about the weather forecast for their upcoming trip. They no longer obsess about their neighbor's barking dog, and they couldn't care less if their coworker is once again upset with them.

After experiencing a life-altering event, you realize that the things we once thought were big issues really don't matter much at all. You've realized that the "before you" was putting energy in the wrong places.

Through immeasurable pain, you have gained perspective.

What Can Be Gained from Pain

I suspect that if you are able to step outside of your pain long enough to examine this idea, you may find that you have gained some deeper relationships. Sometimes, these relationships are with people you would never expect. Maybe your social circle has gotten smaller, but your level of connection with those you have kept near is stronger.

Post-trauma, we value quality over quantity. It's not about the number of people who like you; it's about the few who you feel genuinely value you and can sit with you in the darkness and the light.

Often, after trauma, we develop a greater awareness. You may be more aware of your surroundings. You notice things that wouldn't have registered with you before, like a beautiful sunrise or the length of time in a day (either it runs very fast or painfully slow).

Through

immeasurable

pain, you

have **gained**

perspective.

You see things differently. You may examine the expressions on people's faces as they come out of the grocery store or walk down the street. Whereas before, you might have avoided eye contact or not really paid close attention.

At first, this awareness may seem more like an annoyance for you. You are annoyed that others are joyful. You are annoyed that flowers are blooming. How can flowers bloom when you are in so much pain? Regardless, your sense of awareness has been awakened. Soon, instead of just noticing what annoys you, you will become aware of what makes you smile as well. You may even notice what makes others smile.

With this awareness comes empathy toward others and their life experiences, emotions, strife, and joy. It's not as if we were trying to be ignorant or self-centered before. It's just that most of us travel through life in our own subjective bubble — focusing on what is right in front of us and what tasks need to be completed. In the "before trauma" time, you didn't have the heightened sense of awareness that comes from experiencing a real challenge. Now, you have experienced real strife, which makes you more attuned to others' experiences as well. It also might make you more capable of really supporting them.

FINDING YOUR STRENGTH

The phrase, "You are so strong," is something most survivors hate to hear. They don't feel strong. They feel run over and barely able to manage daily life. While this phrase may make you feel like an imposter, it can also be true. Is it possible that, through this experience, you have become stronger than you ever dreamed you could be before your trauma?

Yes. *You have gained strength!* For some, that means building up the courage to testify in court. For others, it simply means making it through another day so they can focus on making it through the day after that. Why deny yourself the credit you deserve for getting through the challenges (both small and big) that make up this new world you are living in? You *are* strong.

The knowledge you have gained during this experience isn't necessarily knowledge you ever thought you would seek. *Yet, those who have experienced trauma and loss often become experts in things they never anticipated.*

Take this book, for example. If you've made it this far, you've learned about how your body and brain respond to trauma. I suspect you weren't necessarily interested in that information before your trauma.

Maybe you've gained insight into how different systems work. You may now have a better understanding of the medical system, the court system, or the media.

Take stock of the things you have learned and the ways you have applied them in your daily life. Your brain does still work. You are still capable. And a greater understanding of the world always creates greater connections with others.

A Shift in Thinking

If you've ever met me, you know I always say that the biggest gift of my work is the gift of perspective. I feel lighter and less burdened because of this gift. I don't place a lot of importance on things like who won the big game last night or what bill did or did not pass Congress in the latest session. If the Thanksgiving turkey was severely burned? Okay. No big deal.

For some of the people around me, this attitude is hard to relate to. But I work in a field that deals with death. And when you regularly watch people in their most desperate moments, you gain a true understanding of what is important and what is not.

Does this resonate with you? How has your perspective changed since you experienced your trauma or tried to support a loved one recovering from trauma? If you are like the many others I have worked with, you quickly realize that most of the daily minutia we get wrapped up in doesn't really matter at all.

PERSPECTIVE:

- Gives us the gift of appreciation for what really matters
- Strengthens our ability to tune out what doesn't matter
- Helps us develop empathy for others that we didn't know we were capable of

Try this exercise. The next time you are stopped at a busy traffic light, take time to look around at all sides of the intersection. Look at the cars and the people sitting in them. Remind yourself that you aren't the only one carrying a burden or struggling with something heavy. The guy in the car behind you might be as well. And it's likely the person in the car across from you and the one in the car next to them are too. Everyone is carrying something. Just because we can't physically see the pain doesn't mean that others (just like us) aren't struggling.

Pain Can Bring Purpose

Earlier in the book, I mentioned that I lived four miles from Columbine High School at the time of the massacre. I have my own personal story about that day — things I will never forget and emotions I experienced about my quiet little hometown that would never be viewed the same way again. It was ten years later that I first met Susan Klebold, the mother of one of the shooters, Dylan Klebold.

I was an established therapist, attending one of the national conferences I went to every year. It was day two, filled with lots of elbow rubbing and informational sessions from experts in the field of suicidology. As I walked into my afternoon breakout session, I noticed the room was almost completely full. Frankly, I didn't know why there was such a big crowd. I quickly grabbed a spot on the floor and got out my notebook and pen, preparing to listen.

What I didn't realize was that one of the speakers sitting at the table at the front of the room was Susan Klebold. Without identifying herself, she started her presentation by showing us baby pictures. One of the photos was of her toddler son on a tricycle; another was him up to bat playing T-ball. Most everyone in the room couldn't help but smile at the sweet face on the screen.

Moments later, she announced, "My son is Dylan Klebold, one of the two shooters responsible for killing twelve students at Columbine High School."

Everything I thought I understood about this presentation and this woman changed. This wasn't just another lecture. This was real life. This was a chapter of my life unfolding in front of an entire room of my peers. I was dialed into every word that Sue Klebold had to share. What is she doing here? What has her journey been like? And how are people responding to her? In all honesty, I half expected people to boo her or, at the very least, not clap. Instead, she was welcomed with compassion and a lot of curiosity.

REDEFINING SELF

As it turned out, this would not be the only time I would be able to hear Sue speak. She also presented at other conferences I would attend over the years. At the end of each session, I would stand in line to talk to her. I would introduce myself and remind her that I was from Littleton, Colorado. She was always gracious and maybe a little shy.

I started following her in the media and was intrigued by her healing and tenacity. Her story had many more complications and twists than most people cared to hear about. I understand. Thirteen lives were lost, and twenty-four others were injured. Her son was known as a devil. For years, she was chastised and in real physical danger. So how is this woman now standing in front of crowds of people discussing her regrets and her son's behavior and then using this story as a way to advocate for victims?

I'm not sure I ever found the answers to how Sue was able to overcome her trauma and then take on the role she now serves in the mental health community. Still, what she's taught me has been priceless. I learned that through great pain and an incredible clash between a mother's love and deep guilt, she could not be defined as just one thing.

It would be too simplistic to consider Sue Klebold as only "the mother of a mass shooter." She is also a parent, an author, a presenter, an advocate for mental health care, and a mother who has lost a child.

Susan Klebold is an example of a survivor who managed to grapple with a very complicated trauma experience and still find a way to discover and own her new identity. She takes her new reality and the perspective gained from it and uses it to try to bring some good from the tragedy.

▶ After a life-altering event, you realize that things you once thought were big issues really didn't matter much at all. Through immeasurable pain, you have gained perspective.

▶ Gaining perspective can develop deeper relationships, a greater awareness of your surroundings, and a stronger empathy toward others.

▶ Perspective can help us shift our thinking — appreciating what really matters and developing greater empathy for others.

▶ Pain can give you a new purpose in life. Values often change after a traumatic event, and so should our views of how we choose to expend our energy and interest. You might be amazed by what you are capable of creating after trauma.

Mental Health Professionals

When discussing concepts related to identity and perspective, timing is important. This is not a conversation to have with a client who is only a few months out from a traumatic event. I don't often put a timeline on the healing process, so I won't do that here. However, when you feel the client's shock and denial after the event has begun to subside and they have regained some homeostasis, you may want to introduce the concept of the identity narrative and practice exercises that will connect them to their new perspective.

More than likely, you will have to point out examples of perspective to your client. At first, it may not come naturally to them. Don't create false situations to make an experience "brighter" than it is. Instead, listen to their dialogue. When a client mentions something positive, ask them to expand on that particular event.

In time, switch their focus from what they don't have to what they do have. Acknowledge how they have grown. They will need you to point this out for them because they won't often see it for themselves.

Have a client start a log of things that now interest them. This can be useful in identifying the next steps in life. If you hear them speak about passion projects they hope to someday begin, have them add it to the list. Remind them that real purpose can come out of their pain, but only after they've done the work to heal.

Be aware that some clients may want to jump into one of these passion projects immediately. This can serve as a diversion and may slow the healing process. I've seen it happen many times. It is easier to put energy into a project than it is to sit in pain. Encourage them to be patient and do their healing work first. They can't effectively help others until they have first helped themselves.

Chapter *12*

Therapy Tools

Healing doesn't mean the damage never existed.
It means the damage no longer controls your life.

—AKSHAY DUBEY

I wrote *Bulletproof* so you would know, without a doubt, that recovery from gun violence and trauma is attainable. Throughout the book, I've offered suggestions for effective healing, but like you, this is an individual and unique process. How you heal and recover is likely to be different than how someone else does. This chapter is dedicated to diving further into the details of those techniques. You might think of this chapter as the toolbox of the book — a place where you can start when there's something you need to work on or fix.

There is a solution for you. It may be a combination of approaches or just one. In either case, your recovery is reachable, and I'll help you find your way there. While no

Recovery from

gun violence

and trauma

is attainable.

list of therapies can be all-encompassing, the ones introduced in this chapter are a good place to start.

I chose these specific techniques because they are practices and approaches survivors have repeatedly used and relied on. These individuals have described how the techniques have helped them heal. I consider these survivors the experts, not me. I value their opinions on healing far more than any practice I've read about in the latest research journal.

By explaining what these techniques look like, I hope to dispel any fear you may have about committing to the process of doing work to heal. Since it's often the unknown that creates fear, I firmly believe that education calms the mind. I'm preparing you to walk into a new experience.

Healing Stages

Healing looks different for every individual. Maybe your healing means feeling less fearful and regaining optimism about your future. Or, maybe it means being able to engage emotionally with your partner and children again. Your journey will depend on your personal set of goals. These may not match the goals of another survivor, nor should they.

Like every trauma survivor, you are unique. You bring your own life influences and coping skills to the healing process. These experiences, combined with your trauma, shape your healing process, which is likely to occur in three stages:

- Surviving
- Cleansing
- Regaining control

That doesn't sound too overwhelming, does it? By breaking it into smaller pieces, the process of healing feels reachable. The last thing we want to do is set goals that feel impossible to achieve or are too complicated. You'd give up before you even started.

As you begin your healing journey, don't get caught up in trying to meet certain expectations or "getting it right." And don't get too hung up on timing. When it comes to healing, there is no timetable. Instead, just put one foot in front of the other and walk in the direction of healing. You are the only one in control of this healing journey. So, let's begin.

SURVIVING

Many victims who have been directly impacted by gun violence have to conquer the survival stage before they can move forward. For example, In Jennifer's situation, she was tucked away in the hospital, her location a secret in case the perpetrators returned. Hannah was hiding in the corner of her high school's theater for hours, not knowing if there were multiple shooters present. Nicole was worried about her daughter's safety and the safety of her elementary school students, who were also on lockdown.

Although these stories are different, each survivor knew all too well the feeling of being in imminent danger. The fear of that danger can last for weeks or even months after the trauma. For these individuals, the months that followed were focused solely on survival.

What if you weren't directly impacted by gun violence or trauma? What if you were a secondary responder or a caregiver — like Taylor? Do you remember her from earlier in the book? She was the political reporter who was one of the first to arrive in Uvalde, Texas, to report on the Robb Elementary School shooting. She relived the trauma for months, discovering new details as the investigation continued to unfold.

Each news conference brought her emotionally back to the scene. Taylor also needed to learn to survive in a world that she now knew firsthand was filled with violence and injustice.

Like direct victims, the worldview of secondary survivors has also been turned inside out. After witnessing a traumatic event, you may experience real fear or apprehension about what is behind every door. Similar to those who have been directly impacted, your fight-or-flight response has been activated, and your body is in a state of constant alert. You also have to focus on surviving.

CLEANSING

At some point, it's important to find ways to release your trauma. Throughout the book, we have explored what this means and talked about different ways this can be done. Cleansing is part of this process and happens when you talk about, write about, or express the images of the traumatic event that you have been holding in. By sharing your story or your angst, you release some of its hold on you. The cleansing needed to heal can happen simultaneously with the surviving and regaining control stages. It's an ongoing process that will continue throughout your healing journey.

Cleansing is also likely to look different at different times in your healing journey. It may be as simple as sharing your story with a neighbor or friend or writing in a journal when you feel anxious or fearful. It could be creating a blog to share your story with other survivors or sharing your fears with a counselor. It could even be expression through art. The list of possibilities is endless, but the overall message is the same — express your feelings! Find a healthy way to release, express, or expel some of what you are holding. It's important for your physical well-being.

REGAINING CONTROL

Regaining control of your life is the ultimate goal of trauma healing. Following a trauma, it often feels like you are no longer in control of your emotions, body, or thoughts. As the survivors highlighted in this book discovered, regaining control starts when you learn how to redirect your mindset. By taking control of the inner narrative, you gain authority over how the body responds to trauma and moves toward healing.

The techniques described in this chapter will help you regain control of your life, gain control over your trauma, and move forward into your next chapter of life. You've opened this book in hopes of finding relief, and the suggestions that follow can help you get there. You just need to commit to yourself that you will put in the effort.

Effective Tools for Healing

The healing techniques described in this chapter are ones my clients have found to be most beneficial to them. With my support and guidance, we developed individual plans that met their specific needs.

I recommend that you start by finding a caring mental health professional who can guide you through this journey. They don't have to be an expert on all the techniques. If they don't have a specific skill, they can connect you with a professional who does. And that's not a bad thing — the wider your support system, the better.

EYE MOVEMENT DESENSITIZATION AND REPROCESSING (EMDR)

Months after the Robb Elementary School shooting in Uvalde, Texas, Taylor didn't know what to do with the intrusive thoughts that would frequent her mind. When she least expected it, she would envision young children cowering under their desks, waiting for a school shooter to bust through the door. The intrusive thoughts only became more graphic from there. That's when I received a call from her asking for help.

"EMDR? What's that?" I remember the hesitation in her voice as I tried to explain the nontraditional nature of this technique. "I trust you, but this sounds a little weird," she said. I could still hear the confusion in her tone. What I had explained to Taylor was that EMDR is not talk therapy. Instead, it is a non-invasive way of tapping into your trauma, using your own thoughts and memories to get you there.

Eye Movement Desensitization and Reprocessing (EMDR) is different than talk therapy. It is a structured technique that encourages a client to briefly focus on a traumatic memory while a trained EMDR therapist simultaneously leads them through bilateral movements (typically moving the eyes in a pattern). Sounds different, doesn't it? It is. But studies have shown that it is a very effective technique for combatting traumatic distress.

A typical session begins when a client is cued to think of a difficult memory while being instructed to follow a light pattern with their eyes back and forth from left to right. Instead of a light pattern, some EMDR therapists use hand-held vibrating tools that are set at a specific speed to induce the back-and-forth sensation or simply tap a client's leg while their eyes are closed, also in a back-and-forth pattern.

The best way I have found to describe EMDR is this: envision that you have locked the details of your trauma away in a filing cabinet in your mind. You have then locked that filing cabinet behind an iron wall, similar to a vault. You have attempted to tuck that trauma so far away that it can't interrupt your life or shock you suddenly. In fact, if you wanted to recall a memory from your trauma, you would have to first make it into the vault and then unlock the cabinet. In your attempt to gain as much control as you can over your trauma, you have tried to lock away the pain associated with the event, creating as many barriers as possible.

Either by watching the light bar or concentrating on the vibration present in your body, you naturally let some of your mental guards down. Your mind now has to focus on the sensation that is drawing its attention, either the light bar or the vibration. In time, without much protest at all, when cued, your mind will unlock that iron wall and walk over to open the file cabinet. All while being monitored in a safe space by a trained professional. Through the use of this technique, you can finally go through that file of hurtful memories and safely process them or even throw some of them out!

The EMDR process helps to "repair" the mental injury associated with that memory. Remembering what happened to you will no longer feel like reliving it, and the related feelings will feel much more manageable.[21] You aren't hiding it away anymore. You are addressing it head-on. You've taken the power away from a memory that haunts you. You can face your fears and survive.

In fact, EMDR therapy was where I found the greatest relief from my childhood kidnapping. Remember how I described that just the image of a gun in a movie or on a billboard would trigger me? It wasn't until I began working with an EMDR specialist that I was able to see those images and not feel affected. Today, I can watch a shootout on screen or read an article about firearms and not feel the physical impact of a trigger. Instead, I feel nothing! Those images don't hurt me anymore. I have gained greater control over my trauma. And it's liberating.

COGNITIVE BEHAVIORAL THERAPY (CBT)

Cognitive behavioral therapy (CBT) is a type of psychotherapy that focuses on examining the inner narrative we have discussed so much in this book. What you tell yourself is important. It's so important, in fact, that your inner narrative can literally change your brain by creating new, faulty neuropathways (or connections). Those new connections may or may not be true and can lead to faulty beliefs. Some of these faulty beliefs can then lead to reactive behaviors. It's a vicious cycle.

Understanding this cycle exists is helpful, but changing the cycle by yourself can often be challenging. A therapist trained in CBT can help. They use talk therapy to help you identify faulty beliefs and then work with you to make changes in a systematic way.

A CBT specialist helps clients reflect on their thinking patterns and assumptions in order to help them shift away from unhelpful beliefs. Those patterns can be things like overgeneralizing bad outcomes, negative thinking that weakens positive thinking, and always anticipating catastrophic outcomes.

The goal of CBT is to shift toward more balanced and effective thinking patterns. This change aims to restore a sense of control, self-confidence, and predictability, which reduces feelings of fear, the need to escape, and avoidant behaviors.

This reminds me of a young client of mine who had experienced several family losses. By the time he was seventeen, he had lost three of his immediate family members. He had every reason to believe that the world was against him and that his life was destined for misery. In his short years, he couldn't recall living in consistent calm or happiness. All he could recall was pain, sadness, and constant worry. His brain was wired to be on alert and wait for the other shoe to drop.

It took years to convince this young man that maybe life had more to offer him. Maybe it was his turn to experience normalcy and live like an average teenager/young adult. He had been telling himself for so long that life was hard and unfair that he was convinced that he, too, would probably be dead at a young age. He stopped planning for his future because he didn't believe he would have one. He was robbing himself of the possibility of any positive outcome.

Through CBT, we slowly retrained his faulty thinking. With each month that passed, he began to acknowledge that he was still alive and that nothing catastrophic had happened. At first, he was not able to identify this calmness himself. His brain was only wired to acknowledge stress and sadness. I had to point out that his life had been uneventful recently in order for him to recognize that fact.

His mind was only using narrow tunnel vision, so I had to help illuminate all normal aspects of his daily life. Through this explorative talk therapy, I helped to expand his scope.

Then, we took time to examine his inner narrative. What had it been telling him? How much of that message was incorrect? How many other ways was his mind serving him faulty information? With time, I introduced the concept that maybe, just maybe, he could trust the world again. This is only one simple example of CBT. The right practitioner can walk you through effective exercises to help you examine the faulty messages your mind is sending you. You'll learn to identify what is holding you back from new experiences and limiting your future thinking. *Remember, the brain believes what you tell it.*

FLOODING

Flooding is a technique in which a client is directly exposed to a fear-inducing situation while at the same time practicing relaxation techniques. Also referred to as exposure therapy, it is best practiced with the guidance of a trained therapist.

Flooding aims to diminish a traumatic memory's hold on an individual so they can regain control of their story. Exposure to the trauma occurs on the client's timeline with support and structure. Several rounds of exposure may be needed, but eventually, the trigger (whether it's food, a place, an automobile, etc.) will no longer elicit a fight-or-flight response. Overstimulated nerves become calm and deactivated.

A simple example of this process may be addressing a fear of flying. If I had a client who feared flying, we would work together to develop some helpful relaxation techniques. Once the client was comfortable with these relaxation techniques, we would test how well they worked when stressed. I might ask them to simply drive to the airport and park outside — not go in, just park. I would instruct them to use their relaxation skills to stay calm if necessary.

Once they realized that this activity was safe, I would ask them to return to the airport, but this time, park the car and go inside the airport. Again, they could utilize their relaxation skills when needed. This process would continue until my client felt comfortable enough to sit on a plane and take a flight.

As you can see, this type of therapy doesn't happen overnight. It can require several steps. Fear of flying is a useful but perhaps an extreme example. Addressing your fears won't necessarily be as long and drawn out. But it illustrates the way that facing the thing you fear head-on can ultimately allow you to take back control over it.

As I watched several of my clients repeatedly succeed through the use of flooding, I thought about my own trauma and decided that it was time to put it into practice for myself.

Although I was only six at the time of my kidnapping, I remember it well. My family never moved, so I stayed in the same town where the event took place until

I was well into my twenties. I shopped at the mall where the kidnappers had approached us, drove past the street where the gun was put to my head, and used some of the same banks where we were forced to withdraw money.

I was okay with all of these locations except one — the school where my mom and I were dropped off. Although it signaled the end of our horrifying event, this building triggered me. It made no sense, but every time we passed that elementary school, my heart would start pounding, and I would begin sweating. Just being near the school took me back to being six again — small, weak, and afraid. I hated driving past that school. I never shared these fears until years later, when I was an adult. It was my secret.

Now, as an adult, I was ready to face my fears. While on a visit home, I took the car and headed in the direction of the school. I had worried about this for weeks and built up my anticipation of being afraid and uncomfortable.

I drove around the block a few times as I prepared myself, driving in a big circle and then gradually closing the circle with each pass. Finally, I found myself directly in front of the school. I parked and soaked it in. I wouldn't allow my eyes to leave the front of the building. Staring at this place, I took a few calming breaths, but in all honestly, I felt no discomfort or fear.

For years, I had allowed the thought of this building to disturb me. Yet, when I intentionally faced it, I felt nothing. What I did feel was a moment of bewilderment and a feeling of pride! I had just overcome an obstacle. I was continuing to regain control over my trauma.

While this day may sound easy, the process was not. I experienced much of my discomfort and anxiety before facing the actual school building. I had tortured myself for months, which turned into years, with the fear of being near that building. The anticipation of the encounter caused me a lot of anxiety. Remember the bogeyman analogy from earlier in the book? I suggested that it might not be a bad idea to let the bogeyman (your fears) in for a chat. Boy, I wish I had invited him in sooner.

Flooding doesn't have to look like conquering a fear of flying or driving circles around a triggering location. Flooding can also be journaling your story repeatedly. You can pour details of your experience onto a page until you feel that you are diminishing that story's impact on you and who you are. Or flooding can be repeating the story of your trauma to a therapist or trusted friend and practicing relaxation techniques until telling the story doesn't impact you any longer.

The goal of flooding is to dilute the traumatic memories and regain control.

TUNE-UPS

We would all love for trauma work to be "one and done." However, the reality is that trauma work may need to be revisited from time to time. This is true for all survivors but is especially true for those who experienced their trauma in childhood. I call this additional support a tune-up.

Child Survivors — In children, the young brain comprehends the traumatic event differently as it develops. Think of how we change with age. The way you perceived the world at eight years old was quite different than your worldview at twelve, sixteen, eighteen, or twenty-five.

The **goal** of

flooding is

to **dilute** the

traumatic

memories and

regain control.

So, how you remember your trauma at age eight will likely be different than how you remember it at age fourteen and different again at eighteen, twenty-four, and twenty-eight. This is because as you age and mature, your brain can begin to understand the details of the event more comprehensively. You may have more questions yet not feel comfortable asking them because so much time has gone by since the event, and it seems like everyone else has moved on. A tune-up can help you process new feelings and doubts.

It's not usual for a child who has lost a mother to feel confused at eight years old and, at twelve, be sad and envious that they don't have a mom around like all the other kids. Then, at eighteen, they may feel anger that their mom isn't around to see their high school graduation and other accomplishments. I always suggest that parents and guardians be aware of these different stages and consider additional therapy in subsequent years until the brain is fully developed.

Adult Survivors — Adults can also benefit from tune-ups. Even if you have done trauma work in the past, be aware that new triggers may emerge or old triggers might pop back up. *Life is unscripted and unpredictable. You never know when a new event or an encounter that reminds you of the past will bring a flood of emotions to the surface.*

Jennifer, who was shot while in a car, benefited from reconnecting with therapy ... nineteen years after her shooting. Jennifer's first experience with therapy took place during the months immediately after her trauma. She recalls feeling as if they just "didn't know what to do" with her. No one could answer her questions about grief and depression; instead, most of her therapy focused on adjusting to her new disability, not her emotional wellness. She considered therapy at that time a failure.

All these years later, Jennifer came across an article about a colleague who also served on the board of supervisors for Maricopa County, Arizona.[22] At that time, Maricopa County officials were targets of violent threats and harassment after the 2020 election. In this article, the colleague recounted his journey with anxiety and PTSD after months of attempting to manage the national backlash. He revealed that his symptoms had become so uncomfortable that he had sought treatment to help alleviate his distress. He was introduced to EMDR and found healing.

His story was a light bulb moment for Jennifer. She had been struggling emotionally following the January 6th insurrection in 2021. At the time, she was an Arizona state representative and in the public eye. This event retriggered Jennifer's trauma and was a reminder of how quickly life can change. As a political figure, was she also a target? Was Jennifer in danger once again?

She found herself feeling forgetful, disorganized, and angry. The words in her colleague's article hit home for her. If he had struggled with PTSD, sought help, and wasn't afraid to write about it publicly, she could at least give it a try herself.

Jennifer will tell you now that EMDR changed everything for her. It worked so well, in fact, that she at first "didn't trust it." She explains, "Its effect was immediate. I was actually mad at myself. I could have experienced relief so much sooner."

Jennifer's return to therapy and use of EMDR have transformed her life. I think she says it best, "The triggers weren't coming back. The anniversary date of my shooting was no longer filled with dread. The date wasn't different. I was different!"

After your trauma, you will draw from the coping skills that are most effective for you and your lifestyle. But sometimes, we need to re-engage in a structured practice for a short period of time, just until we feel the ground beneath our feet has settled a bit. And there is no shame in asking for additional support. Quite the opposite is true — advocating for yourself is empowering!

fast facts

▸ Healing should be centered around three things: surviving, cleansing, and regaining control.

▸ Eye movement desensitization and reprocessing (EMDR) is a powerful tool that helps individuals combat and regain control over their traumatic event.

▸ Cognitive behavioral therapy (CBT) is a technique that helps rewire faulty brain patterns created by your trauma. A trained CBT therapist will use talk therapy to help you change in a systematic way to create more balance.

▸ Flooding is an exercise in which you face your fears. It involves developing a relaxation practice guided by a specialist. Then, goals are set to help you overcome specific fears or anxiety that are holding you back.

▸ Tune-ups are important in healing work. You may need to revisit healing as your brain changes, develops, and tries to comprehend new information related to your trauma. Additional professional help may be needed to process it. That's okay.

Mental Health Professionals

Talk therapy is not the only solution for all trauma survivors. Some may benefit from a combination of talk therapy and other therapies. The techniques suggested in this chapter are particularly helpful for clients impacted by gun violence or trauma. CBT, flooding, and EMDR are modalities my clients have reported as most successful for them. I always consider my clients to be the experts when it comes to their healing. Remind yourself of the same.

I frequently suggest EMDR for survivors of gun violence, sudden loss, or other trauma. Make a point to explain to your client that this is not talk therapy. If they aren't familiar with this process, explain what they can expect during their first session with an EMDR specialist. If you have not experienced EMDR firsthand, I recommend you try it. It will allow you to gain practical knowledge of the power of the process, which will help you to help your clients.

You can continue to work with a trauma client while referring them to an EMDR specialist. Talk therapy and EMDR are two distinct techniques that can be completed simultaneously. You may find that, in some cases, doing both at the same time might be overwhelming for your client. If so, I suggest taking time off from talk therapy or maybe scheduling your sessions further apart to give your client some relief until their EMDR sessions are complete. EMDR is typically short-term (three to twelve sessions).

It should go without saying, but if you are not an expert in any of the modalities suggested in this chapter, please refer your client to someone who is! There is much research supporting the processes I have discussed. Look into the techniques, consult a supervisor, or connect with a peer to learn more and find local resources.

As I have said before, trauma healing is not a one-stop shop. As long as it's not too overwhelming, your client can work with you while also engaging in other therapies and techniques.

Chapter 13

Helping Yourself

The mind is like water.
When it's turbulent, it's challenging to see.
When it's calm, everything becomes clear.

—PRASAD MAHES

Healing from trauma starts with one small step. After that, you keep taking a few more small steps to move you forward. In the last chapter, I talked about different therapies and techniques that can help you recover from trauma. I likened these to tools you can use as you move toward healing.

The next set of tools we'll talk about are ones you can use on your own. They're day-to-day techniques and practices that will help you reset your system and gain greater control over your trauma. You'll attain acute relief. These are likely to complement other therapies and can help regulate emotional distress. That should sound like a breath of fresh air.

STAYING PRESENT

Living in the present means staying focused on what's happening in the here and now. Staying in the present involves a conscious choice to focus less attention on the future or past by choosing to stay in the moment.

After trauma, survivors can struggle to regulate their emotions, and many spend their days worrying about the future or reliving the past. To combat these erratic emotional waves, many survivors find the habit of practicing mindfulness to be helpful. Meditation is one of the most recognized ways to incorporate mindfulness into daily routines.

I suspect half of you are rolling your eyes right now. And I admit that if someone had recommended mindfulness to me when I was first struggling through my trauma, I might have actually turned my back and walked away. At a minimum, I would have thought to myself, "Well, this person clearly doesn't get it!"

With time, I've learned to be more open to new experiences. I've done a lot of research on this topic, and I've been through the wringer myself and with my clients. Hopefully, I can present meditation and mindfulness to you in a way that explains how it can help calm your nervous system and balance your emotional swings.

In recent years, meditation has gained momentum. Many books have been published about the benefits of meditation and breathwork, and countless studies have reinforced the strong connection between these practices and improved emotional control. These findings suggest that the practice of mindfulness (cultivating awareness and acceptance of the present moment) is associated with healthy emotional regulation.[23] When emotions are managed more thoughtfully, it can result in lower levels of distress, better emotional recovery, less negative thinking, and a better ability to engage in goal-directed behaviors. Read that again. Wouldn't it feel great to complete a difficult task without feeling emotionally run over?

A mindfulness practice is about gaining better control of the mind and overcoming its negative self-talk. I've discussed many times the importance of inner narrative and how these thoughts can create new pathways in your mind. The traumatized brain actually rewires itself. Through the practice of meditation and mindfulness, negative thoughts can be redirected or reframed. The new, negative neuropathways can be changed, and some of the damage caused by trauma can be healed.

In fact, practicing mindfulness goes beyond just counteracting these unhelpful habits. It improves mental health by building more connections between areas in the brain, slowing down reactivity to stress, and increasing the body's senses as a whole. These changes can lead to greater emotional control and can help us better tolerate the ups and downs of relationships and the frustrations and setbacks that life often throws at us.

Trauma-informed mindfulness can be used as a counterbalance to many of the common aftereffects of trauma, including anxiety, the avoidance of difficult memories, reliving the experience, numbing, and feeling easily triggered. Over time, practicing mindfulness can even change and heal the brain. The amygdala can learn to relax, and the hippocampus can return to proper functioning.

Yoga provides another form of mindfulness that may also be helpful. Dr. Bessel Van der Kolk's trauma center has developed a trauma-sensitive yoga practice that has been effective in managing symptoms for both adolescents and adults.[24] Trauma-informed yoga can help you focus on the moment and yourself. It is not designed to take you back to the source of your pain. Instead, it's meant to help you gain awareness of what's happening in your body. Once you have an understanding of what's going on, you can work on letting go of the emotions, stress, and tension that have built up. Yoga also can help you focus on your breath, which can greatly affect your mood.

Something to Note

While evidence supports the use of mindfulness for emotional healing, it is also important to recognize that, in some cases, these practices can cause increased distress.

For some, focusing on being present with their thoughts, feelings, and body can cause unresolved or even undiscovered issues to surface. You may wish to seek out specific trauma-informed mediation practices online or in your area or consult a therapist before beginning.

BREATHE

Breathing sounds like something we shouldn't have to think about, right? Well, yes and no. Remember how I talked about your body taking over during the fight-or-flight response? Without even knowing it, when we're anxious or stressed, we tend to take rapid, shallow breaths that can increase anxious feelings. Breathing (or breathwork) helps you change and improve your breathing patterns by encouraging slow, deep breaths. It calms your nervous system and, by extension, you.

Breathwork is a little different from mindfulness (although they are most beneficial when practiced together.) When the fight-or-flight response is activated, oxygen is sent to your arms and legs in a way that prepares you to fight or flee. Because of this, less oxygen is available for your brain, which makes it difficult to think clearly.

Deep breathing helps direct more oxygen to the thinking part of the brain. Combined with relaxation, this sends a signal to your brain telling it that you're safe. This frees up mental energy to assess the threat.

In my own healing, breathwork has become a common practice for me. I can't count how many times a week I access my deep breathing techniques while at a stoplight or sitting outside of an important meeting. It has changed the way I handle everyday stress. On the rare occasion that I am in real-time need or distress, I know that I can step away from what is making me anxious, sit down for a few minutes, and connect with my breathing. Once I have had a chance to do that, I feel much more prepared to handle what lies in front of me.

Breathwork is simple and available to everyone. Better yet, it can be accessed anywhere. I suggest spending some time researching breathwork techniques. If you are working with a counselor, ask them to guide you through some practices. If you don't have a counselor, yoga and mindfulness centers often offer breathwork sessions. There are also many videos or online classes that can lead through a breathwork practice.

Mindfulness and breathwork can help balance emotions.

HEALTHY HABITS

In addition to the therapies discussed above, here are some words of wisdom that I learned years ago and now live by:

Lack of sleep is the fastest road to insanity. A stressed brain needs rest in order to heal. Waking up each day without adequate sleep is like going into battle without armor. Every day you don't get enough rest, you start the following day at a deficit. Eventually, you are entangled in a never-ending game of catch-up.

Value your sleep above all things. Set an alarm for bedtime so you know when to detach from your book, movie, or social media. Target seven to nine hours a night for as many nights as you can each week. You could also take a power nap (or cat nap) during the day. These short naps last twenty to thirty minutes and are best taken during early to midafternoon. These short rests have been proven to restore energy levels and mental sharpness.

Expectations are the fastest road to disappointment. If you expect to "be better" by a certain date,

Mindfulness

and

breathwork

can help

balance

emotions.

you have only set yourself up for disappointment when that date comes and goes, and you don't feel like you've fully recovered. It doesn't mean that you aren't working hard.

Healing doesn't happen on a precise timeline. It's similar to unrealistic expectations we sometimes have of others. If you expect someone in your life to behave differently than they typically do, and then they don't, that is not on them. You have set yourself up for disappointment. Attempt to rid yourself of expectations. If trauma has taught us anything, it's that there are things we simply can't control. But we can control ourselves and our expectations. Be patient. There is no need to cause yourself unnecessary frustration.

Believe that you can trust the world again. But take it slowly. You have been hurt immeasurably, so of course, you have difficulty trusting others, certain systems, or even the world's plan for you. Try to notice what has gone right in your life instead of focusing on all that has gone wrong. Notice moments when you feel safe or when someone shows up for you. Notice how many days have gone by without receiving devastating news. Consider journaling each night. Start by listing three things that went well. Maybe it's a person who helped you, something you're looking forward to tomorrow, or something you accomplished despite being apprehensive about it. With time, you will begin to realize that bad things happen less often than you may be telling yourself they do.

fast facts

▶ Meditation and mindfulness help focus awareness on the present moment and can help promote emotional regulation, resulting in reduced distress and less negative thinking.

▶ Breathwork helps improve breathing patterns by encouraging slow, deep breaths, which calms the nervous system and recenters you. It can help control your fight-or-flight response and works best when practiced along with mindfulness/meditation.

▶ Mindfulness and breathwork are techniques that can be accessed anywhere, at any time, once you have some simple training.

▶ Incorporating healthy daily habits into your life is something you can do that makes a difference. When combined with other therapies, they can improve your overall feeling of well-being and help you move forward in the healing journey.

Mental Health Professionals

Educate yourself on both mindfulness and breathwork techniques. You do not have to train your client in these modalities, but being familiar with their effectiveness will go a long way in assisting them. Seek out mindfulness centers and breathwork specialists in your area so you are aware of what's available and can offer specific suggestions or recommendations. If you are comfortable and the session permits, I suggest ending each appointment with a short meditation to model this modality for your client. Doing so may help this practice become part of a familiar routine and will send them off in a calmer state of mind.

If you live in a rural community and resources are limited, there are a number of online courses/sessions available. I also suggest participating in continuing education courses that discuss the benefits of mindfulness, breathwork, and somatic exercise. I've included a link to Bessel Van Der Kolk's trauma center in a resources appendix at the end of the book. There's also a wealth of information available online about mindfulness and breathwork techniques.

Chapter 14

You're Stronger Than You Think

Change is painful, but nothing is as painful as staying stuck where you don't belong.

—MANDY HALE

There is an abundance of research showing that a survivor often experiences positive growth after trauma — growth that a non-survivor would not experience. This positive shift is often surprising to survivors, who have become accustomed to struggle, anxiety, and fear. But it is real. Growth can be the outcome of unimaginable loss.

There is a reason this idea is being introduced at the end of the book. If I had come in like a cheerleader at the beginning, yelling, "You've got this, team!" you would have walked away. I would have lost all credibility. I get that.

Growth can

be the

outcome of

unimaginable *loss.*

No one who is suffering wants to be told how fortunate they are for the things they still have. I suspect many of you have experienced that firsthand: "At least you have other children." or "You survived. It could have been so much worse." Or even, "I bet you could sue and win big bucks!" Insert any "you're so lucky" comment here. We've all had someone else try to make us feel better about an adverse situation.

I've always told my clients that someday I will write a book titled "The Stupid Things People Say." It's happened to all of us. And likewise, I suspect that most of us have also, on occasion, made a stupid comment or two. What I'm about to explain is not meant to be one of those moments. Instead, it's meant to show how you *can*, in fact, grow from your adversity.

Post-Traumatic Growth

If you aren't familiar with the term post-traumatic growth, here is a simple definition: it's the positive transformation people can undergo after experiencing trauma. This theory proposes that the way people process trauma can offer them a new worldview, providing them with new insights about themselves and others. Essentially, they have positive shifts in perspective and, in turn, how they see the world.

For some, I suspect that may sound foreign and unattainable. However, research has shown that trauma survivors can, indeed, overcome pain and become more aware of their personal strength. They begin to be able to see new possibilities and experience improved relationships, greater appreciation for life, and deeper spiritual growth. For many, a negative experience can eventually lead to a positive change.

Although sometimes explained in similar ways, post-traumatic growth is not the same as resilience. An individual who is resilient can recover quickly from a difficult situation. Post-traumatic growth is different in that it refers to the positive change that is possible for someone who cannot easily bounce back from a traumatic event or psychological struggle. This process can take a great deal of energy and time, but with effort, personal growth is possible. [25]

A person who possesses the natural attribute of resilience won't necessarily experience post-traumatic growth. A resilient person won't be rocked to the core by trauma and won't have to develop a new belief system. Their resiliency is innate, no matter how deeply it is buried. They will still experience the pain of their trauma; however, they have greater coping skills to combat it. Most often, we see this trait in first responders.

PATH TO GROWTH

There are some common traits in those who are able to achieve post-traumatic growth most easily. They tend to be more open and willing to reconsider their belief system. And they are more likely to take an active role in seeking help from others. Additionally, they have strong social support and are comfortable speaking about their trauma.

While these characteristics can be helpful, there are other ways to cultivate post-traumatic growth. Experts have found several tools that can be used in trauma work to help a survivor reach post-traumatic growth. Here's an overview of some recovery tools. They may sound familiar because we've discussed them elsewhere.

Eye Movement Desensitization and Reprocessing: EMDR is a structured therapy that reduces trauma-related symptoms by having a person focus on traumatic memories while being exposed to bilateral stimulation (eye movements or light bar/vibrations).

Cognitive behavioral therapy: CBT helps clean out faulty, negative thinking that can hold us back from healing by teaching coping skills that focus on how thoughts and beliefs impact actions and feelings.

Prolonged exposure therapy: Similar to flooding, this type of therapy helps people approach trauma-related feelings, memories, and situations over time, working through them safely.

Physical and emotional self-care: These habits help people care for themselves, with or without the help of a mental health professional. It gives them a better awareness of what makes them feel good.[26]

Growth Is Attainable

Post-traumatic growth is something that most trauma survivors strive for. It's a chance to make some meaning out of an unfortunate event that has changed their lives.

It doesn't come easily. However, with the right combination of work, it *is* attainable.

Signs of the post-traumatic growth that we are working toward can include:

- A shift in priorities and values
- More meaningful relationships with others
- An increased sense of personal growth
- An increased appreciation for life, people, and experiences
- A stronger will
- New beliefs
- A stronger spiritual life

Not addressing your trauma can cause additional damage. I know that it may feel counterintuitive to sit in your pain, relive your memories, and walk through your experience again. However, allowing yourself to do so through this work will get you closer to the desired goal of healing.

In time, you may find that you relate to life in new ways. You may value your relationships differently. You may notice that you are thankful for things you never even thought twice about before your trauma. For those who work toward and experience post-traumatic growth, life can have greater meaning.

You Are Different

You are different — and that doesn't have to be a bad thing. Yes, a bad thing has happened to you. But that doesn't

You are

different —

and that

doesn't have

to be a

bad thing.

mean that life, as a whole, is bad. You have been negatively impacted by a traumatic event. Yet, at your core, you are still the person you were before this event. I would even argue that you are a deeper, richer version of yourself. The lens that you view the world through has widened. Trauma changes our frame of reference. Yes, you may have lost things that are important to you. I won't try to candy-coat that. But maybe, at the same time, you have also gained perspective.

Trauma has forced you out of your comfort zone. If you can learn to control your inner narrative, you might be surprised to see some beauty you didn't notice before in places you never thought to look.

WHAT YOU'VE GAINED

I challenge you to think about the things you may have gained. Perhaps before your trauma, you hurried through your day, never taking time to appreciate what you had. Whereas now, you're likely to value simple things in ways you didn't before. You take fewer things for granted. That applies to the people in your life as well. Perhaps you've gained a new appreciation for how they've supported you. And maybe you've begun to put effort into important relationships because you now realize how precious time is with someone you love.

Maybe you have a new focus. It could be that you have found a new purpose, and it is meaningful to you. You may be driven to create change. Having meaning makes all of us better people. Maybe you have found a new tenacity you didn't know you possessed, and you use this drive to fuel your new purpose.

Perhaps you have discovered new strengths — physical, mental, or both. You have had to push yourself harder than ever before just to survive. That does not come easily. Maybe you have been injured and fight every day to regain your physical mobility or learn a new way of living.

You may have gained a deeper understanding of what is important and what isn't and learned to let go of old frustrations and resentments, realizing now that they don't matter. This is higher-level thinking.

Maybe you don't worry about the little things anymore. If the weather is crappy or a package doesn't arrive on time, oh well. You don't spend precious energy and time obsessing over it. You don't try to fix something that doesn't need to be fixed. Because in the big picture — in your new worldview — it doesn't really matter. People matter. That's what is important.

It is also possible that through experiencing your own pain or watching someone else's pain, you've found compassion for others you didn't possess before. Maybe you have become a better listener or have more empathy. You gained a greater understanding that things aren't necessarily always as they appear on the surface. Maybe other people react out of their own hurt. Maybe relationships are damaged by simple misunderstandings. Maybe that guy on the street isn't homeless because he is lazy. Maybe there is more to each story, and if others would take the time to listen and learn, they could also react from a place of compassion.

So, if you are telling yourself that you are weaker, smaller, or wounded because of trauma, you have the power to change your viewpoint. Develop a new understanding of yourself, the world you live in, how you relate to others, and the future that you can have.

You get to choose how to live life now. Just because it's different does not mean it has to be dark!

fast facts

▶ Post-traumatic growth is an outcome. It is the positive transformation people can undergo after experiencing trauma. It is different than resilience, which is the ability to adapt and recover quickly from difficult situations.

▶ Post-traumatic growth comes more easily to individuals who are more open, take an active role in their trauma response by seeking the help of others, and are comfortable speaking about their trauma.

▶ Experts have identified other therapeutic tools that can cultivate post-traumatic growth, including EMDR, cognitive behavioral therapy, prolonged exposure therapy, and physical and emotional self-care.

▶ Post-traumatic growth can bring a greater appreciation for relationships, experiences, and life. It can boost self-confidence and create stronger compassion for others.

▶ You are different. Your trauma has changed you. It has changed how you see the world and given you a new perspective. You can learn to recognize the things you have gained with this new worldview.

Mental Health Professionals

Post-traumatic growth goes beyond resilience. Some people may not only return to their baseline after a traumatic event, but they can exceed it with a positive shift in perspective. This is not a concept that you would bring up at the beginning of a therapeutic relationship. Remember, you need to build rapport and give your client a chance to unpack their trauma, allowing them to tell their story repeatedly, if necessary. This all takes time and patience. It could be that the concept of post-traumatic growth may not be relevant for a year or more.

Trust in a professional doesn't come easily for someone who feels they have just been victimized. Trust should be your primary focus for some time. If you were to start this relationship by reminding your client of how much they have gained through their trauma, you would just become another person who doesn't "get it."

Once the effects of the trauma begin to dilute and coping skills are introduced, you can begin to educate them on post-traumatic growth. This can be quite powerful. Don't be surprised if your client seems skeptical that they have gained anything from their pain. Loss often takes center stage in the beginning. However, in time, you'll likely be amazed at how they start to see things differently after they leave your office.

Make sure to take note of the small things — the rainbow they mentioned when they walked in for their appointment. They are capable of seeing beauty. They may not have even noticed these things prior to their trauma and may need you to point them out. Monthly or bimonthly "growth reports" might be helpful in this regard. Often, patients who are struggling with trauma are not able to see the positive change that has occurred in their own healing. They are too busy trying to make it through each day. Rarely do they have the mental capacity and energy to take stock of where they have been versus where they are now. It will be your job to help them see their own growth.

Chapter 15

Parting Thoughts and Recap

The most important three words you can say to yourself: Yes, I Can!

—DENIS WAITLEY

After one hundred-and-some-odd pages together, I sit at my computer and struggle to find the right parting words. I want to empower you. I want to cheer for you. In all honesty, I want to hug you. All of you. From the survivor to the first responder to the caregiver and mental health providers. What each of you is doing is tough stuff and plays an important role in overcoming and healing from trauma!

It seems like the best use of these last words is to leave you with some highlights. It can't replace the hard work that needs to be done to heal. There are no shortcuts, but the information in this chapter can serve as a reminder of what we've covered throughout the book. It will provide brief summaries of key points, including the science behind how you feel and strategies you can use when you're struggling.

When you need a quick refresher, review these concepts. It can be helpful to know that you have something in your back pocket when you need it.

Three Things to Know

Before we begin our recap, I want you to remember three things. These will help you keep the big picture in mind when day-to-day life may be weighing you down.

- *Don't minimize your role.* Instead, inflate your sense of self. What you are doing – each one of you — is hard work. Give yourself the credit you deserve.
- *Stay true to your course.* The work you are doing on yourself, for a loved one, or for your client can be tiring. Keep moving.
- *Dedicate yourself to the work it takes to heal and grow.* If you need to take a break, that's okay. Just don't forget to re-engage with the practices that benefit you most. You can't get to the other side by standing still.

Keep Moving Forward

What we've learned throughout this book is that healing is not a one-size-fits-all endeavor. It doesn't follow a straight line. In fact, as you heal, you'll sometimes move forward and other times go backward. This is part of the process. Throughout it all, you'll develop personal coping strategies. You'll start to figure out what works for you and what doesn't.

This takes time, help from others, and the ability to trust yourself. I know you're brave because you've survived something terrible, and you're still here — searching for ways to get through the pain.

I also know *you can do this*. Some days, it will be one step forward, two steps back, and maybe even a step sideways. Through it all, you're still working and making progress toward healing.

You Are Not Alone

I wrote this book because gun violence has increased in our society. Exposure to violence has been known to increase rates of anxiety, depression, post-traumatic stress disorder, and suicide. Over fifty percent of our population has reported being impacted by gun violence in some way. People of color in the United States are disproportionately affected.

You are not alone.

The number of impacted individuals is vast and includes not only those who have faced a gun or been involved firsthand in a traumatic event but also everyone who was nearby and indirectly exposed to the trauma. Secondary trauma from gun violence exposure can result in many of the same symptoms.

What's Going On

Trauma biologically changes the way your brain and body function, so you are not imagining that you feel "off" or different. It's common to feel as if you have less control over your emotions. It's also common to feel easily fatigued, both physically and mentally.

TRAUMA AND YOUR BRAIN

Trauma physically impacts brain function. These changes can even be seen on brain scans. This explains why you may feel like you're functioning in a constant state of high alert (or survival mode). It is your body's response to trauma. The fight, flight, freeze, or fawn response has been triggered.

While this is a normal response to trauma, living in a perpetual state of high alert after trauma is exhausting and can be detrimental to your health.

However, these effects can be temporary.

Your brain function can return to what it was prior to your trauma. Like any broken bone or major illness, your brain just needs time to heal. Understanding your body's response to trauma helps you regain control, which is what this book is really about. With the right support, you can regain peace.

You can't control what has happened to you, but you can control how you process it. The goal is to take back control of the narrative.

You **can't** control what **has happened** to you, but you **can control** how **you** **process** it.

TRAUMA AND YOUR BODY

The body and mind are interconnected. Prolonged stress related to unresolved trauma can contribute to serious health conditions.

Unresolved trauma and negative thinking loops need to be "cleaned out." If they're not addressed, they increase stress hormones and impact the body's joints, organs, and muscles. Finding a vagus nerve specialist could help relieve some of the biological response to the stressors of trauma. Familiarize yourself with mindfulness and deep breathing techniques to help alleviate some of the daily stress on your own.

Pay attention to how your body reacts to trauma, and be open to new techniques that could help you heal. Ask others what has worked for them, and think outside of the box.

Regaining Control

Gaining control over our trauma is the key to recovery. We do this by processing it, which often means practicing new therapeutic techniques and stepping outside of old, unhealthy patterns. Consider how you've been responding to your pain, possibly repeating the same habits and expecting different results. Try to replace old patterns with new, more effective coping strategies.

WHAT ARE YOU TELLING YOURSELF?

An inner narrative is the voice you hear in your mind telling you what to believe. These messages are often played on repeat, but they are not always telling you the truth.

Repetitive thoughts, whether positive or negative, create new thought patterns called neuropathways and can change the cognitive process. When a thought is repeated over and over again, your brain starts to believe it is true — even when it may be false. These beliefs could stem from fears, judgments, and/or assumptions.

Worrying has a similar impact. Constant worry wears you down, and studies have shown that what we worry about rarely happens. Researchers call this "worry deceit," and it's the difference between worrying and our reality. Worry deceit robs us of energy and peace.

Your brain believes what you tell it. Choose your words wisely.

TRIGGERS

Triggers can happen often and almost anywhere. They make us feel as if we are no longer in control.

Avoiding a trigger or fear will only prolong its impact on your life. There is no way around this discomfort — the only way out is through it. So buckle up and get started on the work that is necessary to get to the other side. We heal by finding small ways to regain control of our world.

IT'S IMPORTANT TO TALK ABOUT IT

Talking about your trauma is important. Do not attempt to hold on to your traumatic memories to spare others.

Your brain

believes what

you tell it.

Choose your

words **wisely.**

This can create chronic stress, which can lead to a state of imbalance in the body that will not correct itself.

Research shows that chronic stress can create a whole host of negative effects on the body, including an increased heart rate (which can lead to a medical emergency), increased inflammation, a weakened immune system, and increased anxiety.

You may have to ask for what you need from your support system and may have to guide them on how to uniquely help you. That's okay! Trust me, they will be relieved not to have to second-guess what your needs may be.

HOW YOU IDENTIFY YOURSELF MATTERS

How you identify yourself can impact the trajectory of your healing. You are more than your trauma. You get to choose your identity. No one gets to decide for you.

Take control of your narrative. You can be a trauma survivor and also be so much more. Give yourself credit for your strengths. Learn to recognize and pay better attention to what you have gained through your trauma.

Life is filled with memorable moments. Some, we would like to forget. But many of them are pleasurable and filled with incredible joy! These moments each represent a patch in the quilt of your life. One patch does not create a quilt. When put together, all of these patches — the good and the bad — make your life's quilt complete. *Your trauma is only one patch in your quilt of life.*

Healing

When we begin to gain an understanding of the internal source of our personal pain, we can identify how trauma is showing up in our lives, thoughts, and bodies. With that knowledge, we are prepared to identify the techniques that can alleviate symptoms and reestablish a sense of peace in our lives. *Healing does not occur quickly, and it can't be rushed.*

PERSPECTIVE IS A GIFT

With pain can come a new purpose in life. Values often change after a traumatic event, and so should your view of how you choose to spend your energy and interest.

You may find that things you once viewed as a big deal now don't matter much at all. You are capable of creating so much in your life after trauma. *Through immeasurable pain, you can gain perspective.*

POST-TRAUMATIC GROWTH

Post-traumatic growth occurs when trauma survivors find a new sense of personal strength or meaning after a traumatic event. This change helps them live positive, meaningful lives.

Trauma survivors often strive to attain this growth. It doesn't come easily. However, with the right combination of work, it *is* attainable. Allow yourself to be open to this possibility and look for some meaning that has come from the trauma you endured.

HEALING TOOLS

A variety of tools are available to help you navigate the healing process. Everyone's journey is unique to them. Review the chapter on healing tools for a comprehensive list of options so you can begin to find the ones that work for you.

You Can Heal

The reality is that you have changed in many ways. These changes can lead to a greater understanding of what should be valued in life, and they often open your eyes to allow you to see your own strengths — strengths you never knew you possessed.

These changes have helped you to connect with others on a deeper level. They have helped you to love deeper and stand up for yourself more readily. They may even have pushed you to be vulnerable with others and become a more genuine version of yourself.

You see, trauma has changed you and bolstered you to grow. This evolution makes you unique. And in this wisdom gained, you have become more enlightened. You *have* changed, and that can be a *good* thing. This is your "special sauce." Embrace it!

I challenge you to commit to the process of healing, no matter how frightening or exhausting that may sound. You are worth it, and you *can* get through it! The world needs the new, enlightened version of you to share your newly gained appreciation and compassion with others.

reflections

The best way out is always through.
—ROBERT FROST ON HUMAN SUFFERING

Some days are harder than others. At times, we need a reminder of our objective. I wrote this book to become The North Star for your healing journey. On days (or weeks) when you feel like you have lost sight of your goals, review these questions and get yourself back on the right path:

1. *What am I telling myself about who I am today?*
2. *Who do I want to be?*
3. *How have I grown because of my trauma?*
4. *How can I make healing and self-improvement part of my everyday routine?*

Endnotes

1   Giffords Law Center: To Prevent Gun Violence, http://giffords.org.
2   Shannon Schumacher, Ashley Kirzinger, Marley Presiado, et al., "Americans Experiences with Gun-Related Violence, Injuries, and Deaths," KKF.org, April 2023, www.kff.org/other/poll-finding/americans-experiences-with-gun-related-violence-injuries-and-deaths/.
3   "Current Causes of Death in Children and Adolescents in the United States," May 2022, *New England Journal of Medicine,* www.nejm.org.
4   Giffords Law Center: To Prevent Gun Violence, http://giffords.org.
5   Deidre McPhillips, "Gun violence has affected most families in the US, new survey finds," CNN Health, April 11, 2023, www.cnn.com/2023/04/11/health/gun-violence-widespread-impact-kff/index.html.
6   Brooklynn Hitchens, "Second Killings: The Black Women and Girls Left Behind to Grieve America's Growing Gun Violence Crisis," Rockefeller Institute of Government, July 26, 2022, www.rockinst.org/blog/

second-killings-the-black-women-and-girls-left-behind-to-grieve-americas-growing-gun-violence-crisis/.

7 "One-third of US adults say fear of mass shootings prevents them from going to certain places or events," American Psychological Association, August 2019, www.apa.org/news/press/releases/2019/08/fear-mass-shooting.

8 Kerry Breen, "25 Years After Columbine, School Lockdown Drills Are Common. Students Say They Cause Anxiety and Fear — and Want to See Change," *CBS News*, April 23, 2024, www.cbsnews.com/news/columbine-25-years-later-school-lockdown-active-shooter-drills/.

9 Claire McCarthy. "Gun Violence: A Long-Lasting Toll on Children and Teens." Harvard Health, June 28, 2022. https://www.health.harvard.edu/blog/gun-violence-a-long-lasting-toll-on-children-and-teens-202206282771.

10 Michele Rosenthal, "How Trauma Changes the Brain," Boston Clinical Trials, June 25, 2020, www.bostontrials.com/how-trauma-changes-the-brain/#!/.

11 Bessel van der Kolk, The Body Keeps the Score: Mind, Brain and Body in the Transformation of Trauma (UK: Penguin Books, 2015).

12 "Chronic Stress Can Hurt Your Overall Health," ColumbiaDoctors, May 19, 2023, www.columbiadoctors.org/news/chronic-stress-can-hurt-your-overall-health.

13 "Trauma & Chronic Pain," WakeMed, www.wakemed.org/care-and-services/emergency-care/

trauma-centers/trauma-survivors-network/trauma-
your-health/trauma-chronic-pain#:~:text=People%20
who%20have%20experienced%20childhood,can%20
manifest%20as%20physical%20pain.).

14 Michele Rosenthal, "How Trauma Changes the
Brain," Boston Clinical Trials, June 10, 2020, www.
bostontrials.com/how-trauma-changes-the-brain/.

15 Rosenthal, "How Trauma Changes the Brain."

16 "Research Continues on Impact of Trauma on
Changes in Brain," Purdue University News – Purdue
Today, June 8, 2023, www.purdue.edu/newsroom/
purduetoday/releases/2023/Q2/research-continues-on-
impact-of-trauma-on-changes-in-brain.html.

17 Seth J. Gillihan, "How Often Do Your
Worries Actually Come True?" *Psychology
Today,* July 19, 2019, www.psychology-
today.com/us/blog/think-act-be/201907/
how-often-do-your-worries-actually-come-true.

18 Aumyo Hassan, and Sarah J Barber, "The Effects of
Repetition Frequency on the Illusory Truth Effect,"
Cognitive Research: Principles and Implications,
May 13, 2021, www.ncbi.nlm.nih.gov/pmc/articles/
PMC8116821.

19 Kerry Breen, "25 Years After Columbine, School
Lockdown Drills Are Common. Students Say
They Cause Anxiety and Fear — and Want to See
Change," *CBS News,* April 23, 2024, www.cbsnews.
com/news/columbine-25-years-later-school-lock-
down-active-shooter-drills/.

20 "Chronic Stress Can Hurt Your Overall
Health," ColumbiaDoctors, July 27,

2023, www.columbiadoctors.org/news/
chronic-stress-can-hurt-your-overall-health.

21 Professional, Cleveland Clinic Medical.
n.d. "EMDR Therapy." Cleveland Clinic.
https://my.clevelandclinic.org/health/
treatments/22641-emdr-therapy.

22 Yvonne Wingett Sanchez, "Arizona Official
Targeted by Election Deniers Now Struggles
With PTSD," *Washington Post,* May 22, 2023,
www.washingtonpost.com/politics/2023/05/06/
bill-gates-maricopa-county-arizona-ptsd/.

23 Lizabeth Roemer, Sarah Krill Williston, and
Laura Grace Rollins, "Mindfulness and Emotion
Regulation," *Current Opinion in Psychology* 3 June
2015: 52–57, doi.org/10.1016/j.copsyc.2015.02.006.

24 "Mindfulness – Trauma Informed," Trauma
Informed, February 28, 2023, www.trauma-
informed.ca/recovery/phases-of-trauma-recovery/
mindfulness/.

25 Lorna Collier, "Growth After Trauma," American
Psychological Association, November 2016, www.
apa.org/monitor/2016/11/growth-trauma.

26 Nicole McDermott, "Post-Traumatic Growth:
Everything You Need to Know," Forbes, April
28, 2023, www.forbes.com/health/mind/
post-traumatic-growth/.

Acknowledgements

want to start by expressing so much love and appreciation for my friends and family. I disappeared for the greater part of a year while working on this project. Although I was entrenched in my tunnel vision, you showed up for me in ways that I couldn't reciprocate. Your patience with me made all of the difference. It was a beautiful gift!

Big hugs to my pal Jerry for nudging me to write this book and reminding me that I was, indeed, capable when my inner narrative told me otherwise. You are the best cheerleader there is!

Giant high-fives to Niche Pressworks, especially Nicole Gebhardt and Kim Han. Thank you for being brave enough to take this topic on! And a shout out to my designer, Tami, and the entire Niche team for having the vision to represent my ideas so beautifully. Special thanks to my astounding editors, Julie and Anna, without whom this book would merely be a pile of messy ideas sitting on my office floor. Thank you for making me sound intelligent, ladies, and for being as passionate about this project as I am!

To the incredible individuals who were fearless enough to allow me to dig into their stories and use their experiences as examples for others: Without you, this book would simply be hollow pages of words. I am forever grateful for your contribution.

To my husband for always supporting my unconventional work, I don't take that for granted. I know it's not always easy living in my wake. And to my kids, thank you for putting up with a mom who is a therapist. That, in and of itself, is a hardship! Sincerely, my biggest goal in life is to make all of you proud.

Lastly, endless love and gratitude to my parents for providing a safe and loving environment for me to grow up in. Many childhood trauma survivors aren't as fortunate. It made all of the difference in my healing and restored the sense of safety that I needed. I can never thank them enough.

Resources

- Everytown for Gun Safety: Resources for victims and survivors of gun violence
  - ▸ everytownsupportfund.org/everytown-survivor-network/resources-for-victims-and-survivors-of-gun-violence/

- Sandy Hook Promise: Resources and help for victims and survivors of gun violence
  - ▸ sandyhookpromise.org/blog/community-resources/help-for-victims-and-survivors-of-gun-violence/

- Giffords: Toolkit for gun violence survivors and allies
  - ▸ giffords.org/toolkit/from-healing-to-action-a-toolkit-for-gun-violence-survivors-and-allies/

EMDR INTERNATIONAL WEBSITE

- List of EMDR-certified practitioners
  - ▸ emdria.org/about-emdr-therapy/

HEALING MIND AND BODY AFTER TRAUMA

- Trauma Research Foundation – Bessel Van der Kolk:
  - ‣ traumaresearchfoundation.org/programs/faculty/bessel-van-der-kolk/

- For more info on *The Body Keeps the Score*:
  - ‣ besselvanderkolk.com/resources/the-body-keeps-the-score

SUICIDE PREVENTION

- National Suicide Crisis Line – dial 988
- Crisis Text Line - text 741741
- Or access the website:
  - ‣ CrisisTextLine.org

VETERAN RESOURCES

- **Veteran's Cultural Competence:** In-person and virtual trainings aimed at closing the veteran-civilian divide.
  - ‣ mirecc.va.gov/visn2/education/vcc.asp

- **National Center for PTSD**
  - ‣ ptsd.va.gov/

- **Lifeline for Vets:** Crisis management, information, and referral needs for U.S. Veterans and their families.
  - ‣ nvf.org

- **Wounded Warrior Project:** Helping vets transition to civilian life by connecting them to resources and programs.
  - ▸ woundedwarriorproject.org/

- **Worried about a Veteran:** Designated for family members of Veterans on how to have discussions about firearm safety and suicide concerns.
  - ▸ worriedaboutaveteran.org

About the Author

JILL MCMAHON is a licensed professional counselor, speaker, consultant, and gun violence survivor. For over twenty years, she has devoted her career to sitting with people in their darkest moments and helping them heal. Jill's particular focus is on grief and loss. She understands, both professionally and personally, the confusion, pain, and disorientation that weaves in and out of a survivor's new reality.

As a sought-after speaker and consultant, Jill regularly shares her experience and expertise on topics ranging from gun violence trauma to suicide bereavement. She's spoken at conferences, co-written a series of books, and been featured as a favorite podcast guest. She is also passionate about training the next generation of mental health providers and can often be found working with first responders, community organizations, and grief agencies.

When not supporting others, Jill leads indoor cycle classes with the music playing way too loud. Jill married her high school sweetheart and is the proud mom of two wonderful humans. She splits her time between the desert of Arizona and the waters of Maine.

You can find more information on Jill and her contributions at JillMcMahonCounseling.com.

CONTACT

- 🌐 JillMcMahonCounseling.com
- ✉ Jill@JillMcMahonCounseling.com
- 🔗 Jill McMahon
- 📷 @grievewithjill

www.ingramcontent.com/pod-product-compliance
Lightning Source LLC
Chambersburg PA
CBHW061146120626
46546CB00005B/1945